Hjalmar Hjorth Boyesen

A Norseman's pilgrimage

Hjalmar Hjorth Boyesen

A Norseman's pilgrimage

ISBN/EAN: 9783337290931

Printed in Europe, USA, Canada, Australia, Japan

Cover: Foto ©Lupo / pixelio.de

More available books at **www.hansebooks.com**

A NORSEMAN'S PILGRIMAGE.

BY

HJALMAR HJORTH BOYESEN,

AUTHOR OF "GUNNAR."

NEW YORK:
SHELDON & COMPANY.
1875.

CONTENTS.

CHAPTER I.
In Search of a Margaret 7

CHAPTER II.
Retrospect 15

CHAPTER III.
A Day at Wartburg 38

CHAPTER IV.
From Wartburg to Leipsic 56

CHAPTER V.
In Rosenthal 76

CHAPTER VI.
Brother Jonathan's Ball 100

CHAPTER VII.
Ruth's Journal 124

CHAPTER VIII.

The Catastrophe 133

CHAPTER IX.

To the Rescue 151

CHAPTER X.

The Clock Strikes 167

CHAPTER XI.

The Cathedral Tower 187

CHAPTER XII.

The Land of the Vikings 212

CHAPTER XIII.

Ruth's Arrival 237

CHAPTER XIV.

The Glacier Expedition 262

CHAPTER XV.

Conclusion 291

A NORSEMAN'S PILGRIMAGE.

CHAPTER I.

In Search of a Margaret.

OLAF VARBERG had been reading "Faust" since the early dawn. He knew it was not exactly the right thing to do on a Sunday, but Germany had had rather a demoralizing effect upon him, and during his six months' stay in Leipsic the original rigor of his notions about the sanctity of the Sabbath had perceptibly relaxed. It was about ten o'clock in the forenoon. The sun shone brightly, but to Olaf Varberg's eyes it wore a look of perplexity, and he could not get rid of the idea that it was staring directly at him, as much as to say that it was surprised to see him. He leisurely sauntered down the promenade An der Pleisse. The crisp snow crackled under his feet (a very unusual thing, by the way, for Leipsic) and the tall trees of the avenue now and then shook little whimsical showers of hoar-frost down over the hats of the Sunday-dressed idlers. In the middle of the street, people had gathered in groups of fours and fives, and stood gazing through *lorgnettes* and opera glasses at a balloon which was just rising over the house-tops. They seemed to be thoroughly in earnest; their faces wore an air of profound meditation, and they occasionally removed their glasses in order to discuss the phenomenon with their neighbors in a manner which might have led you to suppose that it was a matter of the gravest scientific import. Students with skyblue or scarlet caps, and with deep scars in their faces, lounged up and down the promenade, leisurely smoking their Sunday cigar, and staring impudently at the passing maidens. But Varberg saw nothing of all this. The animated scenes of the street moved before his eyes like an unmeaning pageantry. His lungs seemed still to breathe the mediæval atmosphere of the great tragedy, and with a very pardonable substitution of "her" for "him," he kept repeating to himself this stanza:

> My bosom yearns
> For her alone,
> Ah, dared I clasp her,
> And hold, and own!*

The verse hummed and buzzed in his ears; it exerted an almost painful fascination over him, not unlike the feeling he had had when, on the way across the Atlantic, the propeller of the steamboat, with a nightmarish regularity, had persisted in drumming Richard Rushmore, Richard Rushmore, the name of one of the passengers on board. He had been afraid of that man ever afterward.

Varberg had for years had a passionate yearning for Germany; it had ever been a land of promise to him—the home of art, romanticism, and poetry. "A fair-haired German maiden" had always been his ideal of womanly loveliness and perfection; and now he had been nearly three months in Germany and had not yet found anything which even approached that much-cherished ideal. To be sure, he didn't know many German ladies; but those whom he did know were insufferably dull. Now he must be daring, or take the chance of losing his

* Taylor's translation.

opportunity; he must keep his eyes open, then take a bold step, as Faust did at the church door, and for the rest trust to fortune. Still, Varberg had no intention of giving his love romance a tragic *dénouement;* he was well satisfied to have it end, in the old conventional way, with a happy marriage. "The age of Margarets can certainly not be past," said he to himself, "and that beautiful simplicity which is a peculiar trait of the Germans is a thing which can hardly be overrated in this *blasé* age of ours."

Amid such meditations Varberg had reached the Opera Platz, and was about to change his course toward Rosenthal, when suddenly he observed a young lady crossing the street and advancing toward him. She was tastefully and fashionably dressed, was tall and well formed, but her features were of a clearer, more decided cut than one usually finds in Germany. Varberg came to a sudden stop, and looked at her with an expression as if he were inclined to doubt the evidence of his senses. She dropped her eyes and turned her face away as she passed him. Under other circumstances he would never have thought of pursuing a lady; but in the uncertain glamour of romance which to-day had possessed his mind, he had an absurd sense of his own irresponsibility, and, little heeding whatever scruples might still have been lurking in the depth of his heart, he deliberately turned on his heel and followed close after her down the snow-sparkling avenue. And was she then so strikingly beautiful? Yes; there dwelt in her features a subtle, indefinable charm, which upon Varberg, at least, made the impression of beauty. He could hardly have told, an hour later, whether her nose was straight or curved, but nevertheless the total impression remained indelibly fixed in his memory.

The bells of St. Thomas began to chime, and the young girl hastened down the street, directing her steps toward the church door. Varberg, without questioning the propriety of what he was doing, also doubled his speed, and entered the venerable edifice; with characteristic masculine obtuseness he even imagined himself unobserved, and began to revolve in his mind how he should in the most delicate manner attract her attention, without shocking her sensibility or disturbing her devotions. The grand orchestra was just performing in St. Thomas that day, and the church was consequently crowded. The Leipsickers usually leave when the music is finished, and only a few women and children remain to listen to the sermon. As the crowd in the aisle began to disperse, Varberg looked about him in the hope of discovering his fair unknown; but for awhile his search was vain. A sense of desperate recklessness came over him. "She shall not escape me," he murmured fiercely, and with great strides approached the door at the opposite end of the transept.

Then suddenly he caught a glimpse of a fur-trimmed bonnet, which he thought he recognized, and saw a slender figure almost hid in the shadow of a huge column. It was she; she pressed herself more tightly up against the stone as he drew near, but still she did not appear to observe him; her eyes were steadfastly fixed on the hymn book. His resolution was quickly formed; he slackened his speed, and, as if quite by accident, dropped down into the seat on the other side of the pillar. The congregation began to chant in a sort of feeble, irregular way, and

Varberg felt an irresistible desire to beat the measure with his foot. The fact was, he had no sooner sat down than conscientious scruples woke within him; and as men are apt to do when finding themselves in an absurd situation, he tried to forget one absurdity by venting his energies on another. He did not observe that the people in the neighboring pews were all gazing at him, neither did he see the shocked expression in their pious countenances. "Er ist Ausländer" (he is a foreigner), he heard somebody whispering behind him, and looking up he met the eye of an old gray-headed beadle, who had just entered the pew, and had stopped in front of him:

"Mein Herr," said the man, "this is the women's side. You are disturbing the worship, and I must request you to leave the church."

Varberg awoke as from a dream, jumped up from his seat, and the blood rushed to his head and throbbed violently in his temples. He suddenly realized where he was. Throwing a glance at the other side of the pillar, he saw the unknown lady covering her face with her handkerchief and shaking with suppressed laughter.

"You must come at once," said the beadle, as the other hesitated to obey the order.

The situation was evidently bad enough; and Varberg had sense enough left to know that resistance would make it worse. So, summoning all the calmness that was still at his disposal, he quietly picked up his hat, and majestically marched out of the church. But no sooner had he reached the street than his folly stood before him in all its terrible magnitude. Like a madman he rushed down the avenue, and barely escaped being challenged by a couple of students, whom he ran against without asking their pardon. Having gained the house where he lived, he rang the bell furiously, not remembering that he carried the key in his pocket. The meek little landlady stared wonderingly at him as he slammed the door behind him and breathlessly hurried into his room. There he found "Faust" lying open upon the table, where he had left it in the morning. He seized the book, and in a fit of indignation hurled it against the wall, so that the leaves flew about his ears.

"The devil take all the German Margarets," he cried. "It was the first time I set out in search of an adventure, and it shall be the last."

CHAPTER II.

Retrospect.

FOUR months had passed, and the spring had come. To Varberg these had been long and weary months; and although he had plunged deeply into German literature and philosophy, and made excellent use of his time, he still was painfully aware of the emptiness of his existence, and heartily yearned for something to break its monotony. A hundred times he had resolved forever to banish the Margaret adventure from his thought, and a hundred times he had persuaded himself that he had actually succeeded. Nevertheless he had persistently haunted the churches and the promenades on Sundays and week days, and always with a half confessed desire to catch another glimpse of the fair lady whose first impression of him, he suspected, must have been anything but favorable. He had a vague idea that merely seeing her a second time would necessarily correct this impression; he was convinced that his wishes went no further, and that the fascination which she had exercised over him at their first meeting had been nothing but the whim of a morbidly overwrought fancy. It was all due to "Faust," he thought, and he had carefully shunned the book forever afterward. But now spring had come, and nature was awakening to a stronger and more conscious life. And Varberg too felt his blood running more swiftly in his veins; bolder fancies flitted through his brain, and a vague restlessness diffused itself through all his being. It was the old Norse blood which was stirring, and like his Viking fathers he yearned for great deeds, and planned wide excursions over the land and over the sea. His first choice fell upon Wartburg.

Olaf Varberg was, as has already been hinted, by birth a Norwegian. His childhood had been spent on the fjords of Norway, where the grand solemnity of nature had tended to foster a certain brooding disposition of his mind. Every hill, every stone, and every tree was a monument of past heroism, or at least to his wakeful sense suggested some untold record of the Norseman's forgotten glory. Not a hundred steps from his home stood King Bele's venerable tomb, and on this very strand, where so often he had sat pensively gazing down into the blue deep, it was that Frithjof landed in the summer nights, and hastened to those forbidden meetings with his beloved in Balder's grove; and not very far from the house there was a huge birch, which certainly must have been centuries old. It grew upon a green hillock which the boy fancied looked like a tomb. Here, under this tree, he had spent perhaps the happiest moments of his life. In the long, light summer evenings he would sit there for hours, listening to the strange, soft melodies of the wind as it breathed through the full-leafed crown.

He felt sure that it was a Scald who was buried here; for in the songs of the wind he had seemed to recognize the same strain that had rung in his ears so often, while reading the Scaldic lays in the old Sagas. Then strange emotions would thrill through his breast; he felt that he was himself a Scald, and that he was destined to revive the expiring song and the half-forgotten traditions of the great old time.

When he was twelve years old he had himself written a long poem which he had entitled "The Saga of the Scald." He had only ventured to read it to his grandmother, but she had cried over it for a whole day, and that he felt to be a great reward. His next effort was a tragedy in which the hero was killed in the first act, and was a ghost in the remaining four. His grandfather, in whose house he had been brought up, did not look with so favorable an eye upon his poetic labors, and even did everything in his power to discourage them.

The old Mr. Varberg had had but one son, Olaf's father. But this son had been a wild and unruly spirit, and during his lifetime had been a source of infinite vexation and grief to the worthy old man. The one desire of his mind had been to become an artist; and when his father had refused to furnish him the means for going abroad, he had sold his furniture and his law-books, and had started out in the world as a regular adventurer. During his stay in France he had caught the spirit of the revolution, and had at last returned home full of enthusiasm for liberty and the rights of men. Now the old Mr.

Varberg had always been a stanch conservative, and hated the revolution with all his soul. He was thoroughly convinced that Norway was the freest and happiest land on the earth, and that the existing state of things left nothing to be desired; the son, on the contrary, was never weary of pointing out a thousand instances of injustice and abuse, and his heart yearned to sacrifice life and happiness for the cherished cause of human liberty. Both were strong and determined men, and equally unwilling to yield; and one may easily imagine what must have been the relation of the two under such circumstances.

It is not necessary here to recount the long and manly struggles and the dire failures of the younger Varberg in his efforts to plant the flag of the revolution in the Norse soil. Suffice it to say that one day the sweet face of a Norse maiden sunk deeply into his heart, and that in his marriage with her he found the happiness which he had vainly sought in his unselfish devotion to the cause of our common humanity. He again took up the study of law, was zealous in his supervision of the extensive estate which his father hoped soon to give over into his hands, and promised fair to become the pattern of a husband, and an order-loving citizen. The old man's joy knew no bounds; but he was careful not to show either surprise or delight; he rather seemed to regard the change as a matter of course, and even hinted that he had foreseen it from the very beginning. But little did he know of the combat which it had cost the son thus to abandon one by one the cherished hopes of his youth, and still less did he suspect the ferment which was even now stirring at the bottom of that strong and generous soul. The relation, however, between the two never became a cordial one; they talked mostly on indifferent subjects, and the hopes and desires which lay nearest to the hearts of both they seldom broached to each other.

Then an event occurred which rudely tore the veil from the old man's eyes, and again revealed to him the great gulf which separated him from his son. After a marriage of five years the latter's wife died, leaving behind her two children, Olaf the son, and a daughter Brynhild. It was the love of his wife which had bound her husband to his old home, and had reconciled his large and light-loving soul to a life in a narrow-minded and bigoted society. Now the old restlessness awoke within him; his early longings began to stir in his bosom, and suddenly he packed his trunk and again started out in search of the lost ideals of his youth. But he was destined to experience fresh disappointments. The blind reaction which in Europe had succeeded the enthusiasm of the revolution disheartened and disgusted him, and he was just on the point of bidding farewell to all that his heart held dear, when suddenly the thought struck him that there was still one land remaining which once had received the gospel of liberty with willing ears. And he threw one last sad glance at the old world, and embarked for America.

His children in the meanwhile had remained behind in Norway, and they thrived and grew strong under the ever-watchful care of their anxious grand-parents. The old Mr. Varberg, who prided himself on his name and his blood, took an intense satisfaction in seeing the family features and even its hereditary faults repeated in his grandson. He observed that Olaf had a frank and a generous mind, and this observation was a source of ever fresh delight to him, not because frankness and generosity were morally commendable qualities, but rather because all the Varbergs had been frank and generous. Olaf also had a large nose, which is not generally regarded as a mark of beauty; but the grandfather also delighted in this feature, because he believed that there was a peculiar virtue in the family nose.

The only thing which displeased him in Olaf's character was his tendency to solitary brooding, and his love of poetry. And he feared these traits the more, not only because they had, as he thought, led his son astray, but because in his youth he had been conscious of similar things lurking in some remote corner of his own mind. With him an early marriage and continued prosperity had quelled the unruly longings; but what they might lead to, his son's sad career sufficiently proved. The only artistic enjoyment which the elder Varberg allowed himself to indulge in was music; and he had succeeded in convincing himself that this art was in no way akin to poetry and revolution. He was always wont to class these two terms together.

He had himself a most sensitive ear, and played the violin and violoncello to perfection. Every Wednesday evening he used to gather all the musical *dilettanti* of the neighborhood in his house, and play with them Beethoven's quartets and Haydn's trios until midnight. Olaf and Brynhild were soon needed for the piano parts, and he willingly paid them a quarter of a dollar an hour for practising. Among the boy's earliest recollections were these musical *soirées*, and the strange faces his grandfather made when he played the violoncello.

Since it had become definitely known that the younger Varberg had gone to America, his name was seldom heard in his old home. Only his mother would occasionally refer to something which he had won, or something which he had been fond of in his student days, and would then invariably speak of him only as *he*, with a peculiar emphasis.

"That was one of *his* fancies, too, poor boy," she would say; "he always liked me best in my old *moire antique;* and when that was at last worn out, he would persist in calling all those dresses of mine which he liked *moire antiques.*"

And she would heave a sigh of resignation, and dismiss the subject.

On the days when Olaf received letters from his father, a profound silence always reigned at the dinner-table, until at last the old gentleman would lay down knife and fork and ask, "Is he well?" And Olaf would answer in the same solemn tone, "He is well;" whereto the grandmother would add an "Amen," "God be praised," or some similar devout phrase. Little did the old people suspect what an influence these letters were to have upon the boy's future life. There was a grand sweep and a fervor in these lines which fell like flames into his mind, kindling it to nobler resolves, and wakening to life the good germs which still lay slumbering in its soil. The image of this absent father, with his broad pensive forehead, his thick light beard, and the dark blue eyes with that strange flash in them, still dimly lived in his memory, and it often appeared to him that there was but the helmet and the mantle lacking to make it the perfect likeness of a hero from the Saga's golden times.

Then one day—it was in the year 1862—there came a letter with American stamps on it, which suddenly threw the family into the greatest consternation. It informed Olaf that his father had enlisted as a private in the war, and that he had made arrangements with a reliable friend, who, in case of his death, would write to Norway and deliver his affairs over into the proper hands. "I am happier," he wrote, "than I have ever been before. For I have at last found a cause worth dying for." And in the year 1863 came the letter announcing his death; he was killed on the field in the battle of Gettysburg. A slip of paper bearing the date of the day before the engagement, and addressed to his son, had been found on his breast. It read as follows:

MY DEAR BOY: When this reaches you, the hand which writes it will be cold and dead. My life has been full of error, sorrow, and disappointment, and still I venture to call myself a happy man. For my career has been an unceasing pursuit of that which I have loved above all other things, truth and liberty. And my joy in this moment is the thought that I have a son who will find in clearness that which I groped for in the twilight—a son who will finish the work which I have left undone. I am convinced that America is the land of the future, and in spite of injustice, abuse, and corruption, there is health and strength enough in this nation to lift the whole world; I mean to raise it to a higher view of itself, and of the destiny of mankind. Therefore my last prayer to you is, that you should, as soon as you have finished your college course, embark for New York, and spend one year here, travelling about the country, and making yourself acquainted with its people and its institutions. If you write to my friend Dr. C——, in Boston, he will furnish you with money. I have left five thousand dollars for you in his hands. I feel as confident that you will fulfil this my last wish as if I had your spoken promise. If at the end of a year you prefer to return to Norway, you will at least return a wiser man than you left; if you decide to remain, God will also find a work for you to do here. I rely upon His guidance. Here on the broad arena of life you are nearer to the world's great heart, and hear with joy its mighty pulsations; the horizon of your mind widens, the grand possibilities of your nature develop faster, and you become a larger and a stronger man.

I have a presentiment that my life is drawing to its close. But if, as God grant, you grow up to be a noble and liberty-loving man, I shall live in you and in your children. Farewell! God bless you.

Your loving
FATHER.

Olaf did not show this letter to his grandparents. It is needless to say that it made a deep impression upon him; he hid it in his bosom, and carried it there ever afterward. A few months later he entered college, and soon became the leader of the democratic faction among the students. His eloquence and his winning manner, as well as the high standing of his family, made him welcome everywhere, and he gained access to the best society of the capital. But amid all the noise and gayety of these years the solemn voice of his dead father seemed to call to him from afar, and to remind him of the great responsibility which rested upon him. In the summer vacations he returned home, and spent the long bright days rowing about on the fjord, dreaming of the past, and maturing his plans for the future. Fate had placed him in a strange position, and he often violently accused himself and felt as if he were a traitor; for he could not confide to his grandparents, whom he owed so much, that which was stirring within him; and to abandon his resolution would be treason to his father's memory. And when restlessness and unhappiness oppressed him, he poured forth his soul in song, and his songs touched the hearts and gained him no small reputation among his fellow students.

Then at last came the terrible day, when, after having graduated with distinction, he returned home, pulled from his bosom the fatal letter, and unburdened his heart. His grandmother wept and sobbed; then took medicine and went to bed; called him cruel and ungrateful in one moment, and in the next her own dear, blessed child. But his resolution was formed, and he remained firm. His grandfather's grief was not so noisy; but it was deep and genuine, and Olaf once came very near yielding; for it was painful to see the old man sitting there so pale and distracted in his chair, and then, as soon as any one entered the room, waking up suddenly and make a desperate effort to appear cheerful and unconcerned. One thing, however, Olaf was induced to promise, and that was to remain at home during the winter, and to defer his journey until spring. The household soon again lapsed into its usual routine, and the subject which had lately agitated it seemed to have dropped out of every one's memory. But what is hidden is not forgotten, says a Norwegian proverb; and Olaf did not fail to detect a secret uneasiness which manifested itself in an over-anxious care for his comfort, and in the somewhat strained efforts on the part of the family to amuse and distract him; and one of these efforts, although indeed it had for its object a more serious thing than amusement, is perhaps worthy of being recorded.

One of the most zealous participants in Mr. Varberg's muscial *soirées* was the old Colonel Haraldson. He was, next to Mr. Varberg, the wealthiest man in the parish, and had an only daughter, Thora, to whom Olaf had in his boyhood addressed numerous sonnets and serenades. Miss Thora was a pretty, fair-haired Norse damsel, and had on her part shown no disinclination to become the object of the young man's admiration. During his college years she had been rather more shy and reserved in her manner toward him, which his grandmother regarded as a very favorable sign. And now, when it was needful at any price to keep her boy from running away from her, she—the old lady—determined to take advantage of this early romance, and with his sister's aid she planned a little campaign against him.

Thora had always been Brynhild's bosom friend, and there could consequently, to outsiders, be nothing remarkable in her coming almost daily to the parties and musicals at the Varberg mansion. Olaf, who was wholly unsuspicious, readily ran into the snare, and was easily beguiled into sleigh-rides and excursions by land and water, on which the two young ladies invariably accompanied him. At the parties, which at this season were very frequent among the officials and landed proprietors of the parish, he was always chosen the director of the evening, and at his sister's request he never refused to " open the ball" with the Colonel's daughter. Thus the winter passed, and if Olaf had not been too absorbed in his plans for the journey, he could not have failed to observe that Thora's eyes shone with a softer and tenderer light whenever they met his, and that a serene, maidenly joy beamed from her countenance whenever his arm encircled her in the dance. But indeed Olaf had too much to think of, and he perceived nothing. The great unknown world lay before him in the shimmering light of a dream, in which the objects appeared larger and of grander proportions, until even his own person began to assume the dimensions of a hero, and the voyage he was about to undertake became a daring cruise, like those of the Norse Vikings in the romantic days of old; and in such a mood renunciation is easy.

One morning in March Olaf woke up late, after having spent the greater part of the night dancing at the Colonel's. He was not a little astonished to find his grandfather seated at his bedside, and looking at him with an expression of almost motherly tenderness in his features. He had evidently been sitting there for a long while. "Well, my boy," said the old man, "you have slept late this morning. Youth has need of sleep." Olaf yawned, and murmured something in reply.

"I have come," continued the other, "to tell you how gratified I am to know that you have finally made up your mind in regard to the matter in which we are all so much interested."

Olaf opened his eyes wide and stared in amazement at his grandfather. Could it be possible that the old man would give his consent to the journey, and let him depart in peace?

"Your grandmother has told me all about it, and indeed it has made me feel at least ten years younger. Thora is an excellent, sensible girl, and she belongs to one of the best and oldest families in the country. You know that I am willing to give up the house to you at any time you may wish; or if you should prefer a house of your own——"

Olaf, with an utterly bewildered air, raised himself on his elbows and tried to collect his senses. A vague sensation as if a great misfortune had befallen him, shot through his brain. Was it possible that he had proposed to Thora without knowing it? He indeed remembered that some such thought had haunted him yesterday during the waltz; and had she now come and presented herself to his grandparents as their daughter-in-law?

Old Mr. Varberg in the meanwhile became impatient, and began to pace up and down the floor.

"Well, my boy," he exclaimed, "you don't seem to be quite awake yet, or can it be possible that you are not pleased?"

"Indeed, grandfather, I should think she might have waited until I got up and could have come for her," cried Olaf, answering his own fear rather than his grandfather's question. "And to tell the truth," he added in a voice of comic despair, "I don't understand a word of what you are saying. I haven't made up my mind about anything, except that I am going to America; and if you will give your consent to that, I shall be very much obliged to you."

"My dear child," retorted the old man rather vehemently, "either you are dreaming or I am

—or—or your grandmother. I must utterly have misunderstood her."

And so saying he rushed out of the room. It would be tempting to rehearse the young Viking's debate with himself while he dressed that morning. The first vision that stole into his fancy was that of Thora in her airy, sylph-like ball-costume; he saw the tender glance in her eyes, saw the sweet temptation of her lips, and the golden cross around her neck, which glittered and rose and fell with the movement of her bosom. In the next moment he half persuaded himself that he had actually whispered some tender word in her ear, as she leaned on his arm in the waltz; that he had proposed to her on the staircase and kissed her in a corner, just as they carried away the ice cream; and finally that she had promised to call in the morning, but would tell nobody what had happened except Brynhild. And now Brynhild had evidently, after her manner, taken the rest of the family into her confidence.

While diverting himself with these and other possibilities, he finished his toilet and went to the window to raise the curtains. It was about noon, and the sun shone brightly into the room. The sea dashed against the pier, and down on the strand the waves brawled in loud-voiced chorus. The Viking longings again awoke, and Thora's beauty and loveliness looked pale as the foam upon the beach. It was all a dream, and as he reviewed the events of the last months he saw the whole plot, and he owned that his grandmother had played her cards skilfully. The old heroism asserted its rights within him, and the pleasing fancies of a moment ago were now but delusions and deceit. And still (shall I confess it?) in some corner of his heart there lurked a vague regret that it had not all been true and real.

"Good God," he cried, as he slammed the door after him and walked down to breakfast—"Good God, what a brute I am!"

This consciousness, however, did not in the least influence his actions; that same day the battle was fought, and the end of it was that his grandmother had to quit the field, and his grandfather, seeing that resistance was vain, likewise yielded.

In the beginning of April, Olaf bade farewell

to his native valley. Thora refused to see him when he came to call upon her; but the evening before he sailed she probably relented, and she met him "by accident," as he was taking his walk; and if rumor be true, she cried over him and kissed him good-by.

How a man of Olaf's fantastic spirit, and with his latent romantic tendencies, would fare in a land like America, is not difficult to conjecture. Most people at first did not know what to make of him, but still were kind to him, because they found him entertaining and liked to exhibit him as a curiosity. The fault, however, was his no less than theirs. He made no effort to throw off or even to step out of his narrow national shell, and they did not meet him half-way and thereby make the approach easier. And in his dreary solitude Olaf sought refuge from the world in his old talent, that of song. He often wrote night after night, until the dawn surprised him; the memories of the fjord and the valley of his childhood returned to him in the silence of the night; the loors* echoed between the moun-

---

* A *loor* is a long wooden horn, wound with birch bark, which the peasants use to call the cattle home in the evening.

tains, the Neck played in the cataracts, and the clear cattle-bells made the air alive with music. The unambitious story which had been thus commenced only to ease an overburdened mind, gradually grew under his hands, until the thought struck him that it might perhaps find a publisher. And a publisher was found.

Varberg spent many a delightful hour in conjectures as to the probable fate of his work, and in constructing ingenious theories regarding its influence upon the future of American literature. The possibility never occurred to him that it might fall dead from the press, and leave no more trace behind it than the bubble that bursts on the sea. Still, whatever its fate may have been in the great world, upon Varberg himself it did produce a most marked effect. It taught him to look upon himself as a man of letters; it revived all the early dreams of his childhood, concentrated his energies, and clearly defined the aim and object of his life.

And strange to say, this book also changed his relation to the land of his adoption; the praise of those whose opinion he valued was grateful to him, and the readiness with which they recognized the possibilities of his nature, and accepted the promise of his youth and talent, touched his heart. He became in a short time an enthusiastic American; his father had, a few months before his death, assumed American citizenship, and Olaf was agreeably surprised to find that, according to the laws of this country, he had himself for some time been enjoying the same honor without being aware of it. Therefore, when at the end of five years his grandfather wrote and implored him to pay a visit to his old home, if only for a few months, he was inclined to look upon this journey as a kind of literary pilgrimage, and consequently willingly assented. At Christmas time he sailed for Hamburg, but as communication with Norway at that time of the year was difficult, and moreover he preferred to see his native land in its summer glory, he immediately proceeded to Leipsic, where he intended to spend a few months at the University; and it is here where we have the pleasure of making his acquaintance.

CHAPTER III.

A Day at Wartburg.

IT was in rather an elegiac mood that Mr. Varberg left Leipsic for Weimar and Eisenach. As the so-called express train slowly wound its way up through the lovely Thuringian valley, he had abundant opportunities to watch the soft, vague beauty of a German summer day. Between Leipsic and Weimar the country can hardly be called beautiful, but a June day is lovely everywhere; and as the generous sky lent its changeful tints of rose and purple to the wide plains and the stiff, soldier-like planted forests, which look like Prussian regiments on parade, their picturesque barrenness assumed an air of tender regret, like a plain Cinderella that mourns the lowliness of her estate. And Varberg was just in a mood to appreciate a tender suggestion; for in some hidden recess of his heart the half-confessed yearnings were still breathing their faint melodies in tones as vague and as sweet to his ear as those of a wind-tuned Æolian harp. He dared not think it, but nevertheless he cherished the suspicion against himself that he was fleeing from Leipsic because its very air was filled with the presence of the unknown Margaret. " Love is a disease," says Tourguéneff. " And a contagious one," added Varberg in his thought. " It is like the cholera; it is in the air we breathe, in the water we drink, and imparts itself with equal ease through any and all of our senses."

Varberg spent three days in Weimar; visited the Museum, the Grand Ducal Library, the Palace, etc. Long he lingered in Schiller's rooms, where, to his astonishment he found a large portrait of Abraham Lincoln; and through a stratagem he even gained admission to that forbidden sanctuary hallowed by the memory of " Faust's " great author. It is needless to recount here his exploration of the ruined castle of Rudolfsburg. Goseck, Schönburg, the Cathedral of Erfurt and the Thuringian valley are familiar to every traveller. On the evening of the fourth day he reached Eisenach. It was already dark, and having engaged a couple of rooms in "The Grand Duke of Weimar," he started for the Old Town, and strolled aimlessly about for an hour, lost in romantic speculations.

The following morning he mounted the cliff on the brow of which the old castle of Wartburg is situated; spent a couple of hours in the grand Sängersaal and in Luther's cell, and finally toward evening started out in search of the famous Venusberg. According to the legend, the old Roman goddess, after having been banished from the world by Christ, has sought refuge in this mountain, and here her sweet voice may still be heard through the forest silence when she sings her pagan songs, and lures Christian knights to destruction.

The red sun hung low over the western mountain ridges; a soft purple mist hovered over the tops of the forest, and a slumberous perfume, as of a host of invisible flowers, was wafted upward on the breeze. Varberg stood before a large, thickly wooded hill, at the base of which a labyrinth of narrow pathways wound in and out through gloomy coves and arbors. A chorus of unseen waters filled his ears with its faint, delicious rushing, and its subdued ripple calmed his troubled soul like the crooning of a distant lullaby. Something told him that this must be the Venusberg; he threw himself down on the ground, and began to gaze up into the sky, which flowed on like a broad blue sea between airy islands of cloud. The great linden trees rustled with their leaves, and a faint tremor ran through the air, like a vague, expectant whisper. And the longer he listened the more strongly his mind became possessed of an irrational desire to see, if but for one moment, the phantom of the ancient legend embodied in living flesh and blood. It was a desire altogether independent of belief—a mere regretful wish that all these delightful mysteries might once more be real as in times of old. Then—could he trust his senses?—there was a creaking in the copse hard by, and he heard the sound of light, hurried footsteps.

He quickly raised himself on his elbows, and and discovered the outlines of a maidenly figure shimmering through the leaves. The boughs were bent aside, and a beautiful young face appeared for a moment, and with an exclamation of fright, again vanished. Utterly bewildered, Varberg sprang to his feet; he ran his hand over his eyes, and vainly tried to collect his thoughts. That face was only too familiar to him; it was the very face which for months past had been haunting his fancy; it was the face of his Margaret. Looking toward the copse where he had seen her vanish, he discovered a red and white shawl, which in her fright she had let fall. He picked it up, and began to ascend the hill. The blood throbbed in his temples, and he hardly felt the touch of the earth he was treading. Having gained a point where he had a free view of the forest below, he sat down on a stone, and with his eye followed the course of the intertwining footpaths. Presently he saw something white which fluttered between the trunks of two huge beeches, a few hundred feet away. He arose and hastily made his way to the spot. It was again the mysterious maiden. She had either fallen, or from exhaustion let herself drop on the ground. Her whole frame trembled, and she panted violently.

"Pardon me," began he.

She started with a faint cry at the sound of

his voice, then quickly collected herself, and made an effort to rise.

"I hope you will forgive me," continued he, "if I have involuntarily been the cause of your fright. A hundred times I beg your pardon. You left your shawl down on the hillside. I picked it up. Here it is."

He handed her the shawl, and half mechanically she stretched out her hand to receive it.

"Thank you," she whispered.

"If I can be of any service to you," said he after a pause, "I hope you will not hesitate to let me know."

There was something so hearty and honest in the way he spoke, that her fear gradually vanished, and as his eye met hers he saw in it a rapid gleam of recognition, to which he unconsciously responded.

"I know it was very foolish in me to be frightened," she said, with a feeble attempt to smile. "But I have lost my way, and this is the Venusberg, you know, and it is all so strange, so strange."

"I suppose you wish to return to Eisenach?"

"Yes; I started for the castle this morning,

with my cousin. She had no curiosity to see the Venusberg, and so I went alone. I am to meet her again in Eisenach this evening. You know," she added apologetically, "that American ladies have the privilege of doing things which Europeans call strange; and when they are abroad they are somehow thrown off their responsibility, and they often do things which would hardly occur to them if they were at home."

Varberg had crossed his arms over his breast, and stood leaning up against the trunk of a tree. "Aha," he thought, "then my fair Margaret is an American. An American Margaret! What an absurdity!" And he was not sure but that in his heart of hearts he cherished a vague resentment against her for her unwillingness to identify herself with the romantic being his fancy had made her. Her cheeks were still flushed, and there was a glimmer of uneasiness in her dark eyes; her mouth and chin were exquisitely sculptured, her nose slightly Roman, and her hair of a dark brown hue, which lacked but the fraction of a tinge of being black. The magnificent turn of her shoulders, the fulness of her bust, and the grand poise of her head gave her an air of self-confidence and repose, and even in the midst of her agitation, she preserved a certain statuesqueness of manner and bearing. Somehow, the suddenness and mystery of their meeting put them more readily at ease with each other than if they had met in the conventional way in a crowded drawing-room; and having by her look been assured of her confidence in him, Varberg sat down in the heather at her feet and began to talk with her about the history and the legends of the place. She answered at first a little timidly; then, unconsciously yielding to the fascination of the place, she grew more communicative, and before an hour had passed they found themselves talking together as if they had known each other for years. Still, there was a vague look of solicitude, as if she were afraid of having done something wrong, when finally she rose to bid him farewell.

"I shall have to continue my wanderings,' said she, "if I am to reach the city before dark. Perhaps you would kindly start me on the right road."

"I am myself going to Eisenach," answered

he, "and if you would trust yourself to my guidance, I should deem it a favor."

"When I think of it," said she hesitatingly, "I fear I have no alternative. I have not the faintest idea of where I am."

The sun had in the meanwhile sunk behind the borders of the forest, and the golden crescent of the moon sailed calmly through a limpid ocean of blue sky. The air was so soft and warm, the evening breeze so gently caressing, and the whisper of the leaves so deliciously vague and soothing, that mere existence seemed a luxury. The air was filled with the fragrance of fresh sprouts and flowers; the dim shadows of the trees quivered mysteriously in the moonlight, and the clear flute-notes of the nightingale enlivened the gloom of the beech copse.

"It is on a night like this that the elf maidens tread the dance," remarked Varberg, as he helped his companion down the side of a moss-grown rock.

"Elf maidens? What are elf maidens?"

"They are the ghosts of dead flowers."

"The ghost of a flower! I never heard of such a thing."

A Day at Wartburg. 47

"That is the consequencce of your American education."

"That is very possible. But I am willing to be instructed. You seem to be a perfect encyclopædia of mythical lore. Tell me why the elf maidens dance, and why they dance just on a night like this."

The road was now becoming smoother, and while they walked along under the moonlit dome of the forest, he told her the legends of gnomes, elves, and nixies that inhabited the mountains, groves, and rivers of the old world.

"And don't you think they could be induced to emigrate to America?" she asked with a merry laugh. "We need something of the kind, especially about Boston and Cambridge, where the transcendental tea meetings are in danger of reducing us all into mere abstract entities or nonentities, and I don't know what it is all called."

"We get so many less desirable elements from Europe," he replied gravely. "It would be well if we could also import some of her noble poetry and romance."

"Yes, indeed; I perfectly agree with you.

Only think of it! To have Mr. Sphinx of Concord digging in his garden, and suddenly bringing to light a century-old gnome, who sternly calls him to account for disturbing the sanctity of his subterranean home, and prophesies that, as a penality, his race shall be extinct in the third generation; and Mr. Jockey, of the Lane Street Church, bathing in the Charles River, to wash off the dust of a horse-race, being clasped in the cold embrace of a lovely mermaid. And to complete the picture, I should like to see the Rev. Mr. Buddha taking an evening walk (if he is addicted to that sort of thing), and being abruptly confronted by a group of airy elf maidens, who wind their white arms about him and force him to dance a moonlight jig with them to the music of harebells and lilies o' the valley. Ah, I think I see the surprise of the reverend gentleman," she added, laughing heartily. "I would give a good deal for the chance of looking on."

Varberg, although he was slightly shocked at her lack of reverence for the old traditions, could, not help joining in her gayety; and he owned that he would himself enjoy seeing the great transcendentalists in similar situations.

"I could very well imagine Lowell catching glimpses of elves and fairies under his tall elms in Cambridge," he remarked. "In fact, I have no doubt that he often does."

"Yes; there is something of the old world about Lowell," she replied. "Since I read those wonderful opening pages of his 'Cathedral,' and that charming essay, 'My Garden Acquaintance,' I do believe him capable of seeing things which are hidden from the sight of us ordinary mortals. And the experience of to-day, this moonlight ramble under the shadow of ancient Wartburg, and your mythical tales, have affected me so strangely."

There was to him a glamour of unreality about the incidents of this day, and he could hardly, even at this moment, persuade himself that he was treading on solid earth. It was a peculiarity of his mind that it wandered off, on the slightest provocation, into all sorts of dreamy vagaries, and now it was this very maiden, whom his fancy had clothed with all the attributes of romance, who sternly rent the veil, and by her realistic talk forced him to accept her in her true character. She was evidently not deficient in fancy, but she was a true product of American soil, and she represented those very qualities which he especially disapproved of in Americans—their realistic humor and their utter irreverence for tradition.

They had reached the place where the railroad bridge overarches the road, and Varberg was just indulging in a mental denunciation of railroads, when the girl again broke his reverie:

"How charmingly impersonal our talk has been," she exclaimed. "This is the second time we meet—I mean we have spent several hours in each other's company, and you have not yet told me your name."

"My name is Olaf Varberg."

"Olaf! What a delightfully barbarous name! I beg your pardon; I only intended to say that it was a very unusual name."

"It is a Norwegian name. I am by birth a Norwegian and by adoption an American."

"My name is Ruth Copley; and I need not tell you that I was born in Boston, since you must already have inferred that from my talk. I have spent about a year in Leipsic, studying music at the Conservatory."

This called for a similar confidence on his part; and before they had entered the streets of Eisenach, they were both acquainted with a good many incidents of each other's lives. The sag-roofed, turf-thatched cottages in the outskirts of the town, with their queer little window panes, gazed upon them with a ghastly stare from out the moonlit stillness, like that of an eye which remains open in sleep. The footsteps of the two wanderers echoed sharply between the walls of the stone-paved courts, and their black shadows travelled silently and swiftly at their sides.

"Oh, what a horrid place!" said Ruth, unconsciously pressing herself more tightly up to her companion.

"Do you know the legend of the Willies?" asked he.

"Not N. P.," she replied with a forced smile. "I don't know any other Willis."

"It is an Austrian legend. The Willies are dead brides—maidens who have died between the betrothal and the wedding; and on a summer night like this, when the city is silent—"

"How terrible!" and she shuddered violently.

He paused and looked inquiringly into her face.

"I thought you did not believe in ghosts and legends," an evil demon whispered in his ear, and he was ungenerous enough to utter the words.

"Ah, that is cruel," she exclaimed. "I admit I do prefer to see the new moon over my right shoulder; but ghosts—no, I do not believe in them. And now you shall finish your legend, or I shall not stir from the spot. It was on a summer night like this, you said—"

"Miss Copley, pardon me. I had no idea—"

"Yes; when you have finished your legend," she interrupted him. And she stood tall and calm, with the light shawl flung toga-like about her shoulders, while the pallid moonlight, as it were, lifted and etherealized her divine form. Varberg's first impulse was to throw himself at her feet and madly declare his love for her. Then suddenly it struck him that this would make a capital scene in a story, and the heroic spirit immediately departed.

"Well, since you demand it," retorted he, in a somewhat injured tone ('and who would have imagined that she could be so obstinate,' he added in his own mind), "these ghostly brides glide at midnight through the empty streets, and if a young man comes in their way, they wind their lily arms about him, and onward they float, with wilder and ever wilder movements, and the unhappy wanderer is forced to follow. Then their phantom-like beauty lures his senses; he begins to feel the spell of the dance; he returns their caresses, and embraces—death."

"Girls always remain faithful to their character," she observed, after a minute's silence. "A phantom flirt! What a curious idea!"

They both lapsed into silence. The legend of the dead brides evidently occupied Miss Copley's fancy more than she would own; for as they stood under the vault of the wall which separates the New Town from the old, she was visibly startled at the sound of his voice, and barely comprehended what he was saying.

"In what hotel are you stopping, Miss Copley?"

"What hotel—Ah, the Grand Duke of Weimar."

"Then we are happily housemates."

In the parlor of the hotel they found the cousin, Miss Bailey, who embraced and kissed Ruth, and declared that she had supposed she had been dead a million times. Miss Bailey was small of stature, and was as fair as her cousin was dark; her plump round face, her pouting lips, and her frank blue eyes had something amusingly innocent about them, almost babylike. There was a certain childlike vehemence in her manner as in her speech, provoked, as Varberg fancied, or rather exaggerated, by the fact that she seemed herself to be conscious of it. At the supper table her guileless eyes, half unknowingly, appealed to him in a way which implied no small degree of confidence, and when his were rather slow to respond, she shrank back with a puzzled frown, and held her peace for the next ten minutes. Then, gradually divining her character, he did her penance in his heart, and again the innocent blue eyes beamed forth their ready forgiveness. When the supper was finished, he bade the ladies good-night, and retired to his own room, pulled off his coat and flung himself into an easy chair. A strange torpor had come over him; a hundred thoughts whirled about in his brain, and floated in a nebulous procession before his eyes.

"Do I really love her," he murmured to himself, "or is it merely imagination? I have imagined myself in love with at least twenty women, but it usually passed off in the course of a fortnight."

He went to the window, thrust it open, and leaned out over the sill. His eyes instinctively wandered upward, and in the window right above him he caught a glimpse of a maidenly form in a light *negligée;* her long, dark hair was loosened, and hung in rich profusion down over her shoulders, and her face was turned toward the starlit sky. He must have made a noise with the window, or in some way betrayed himself, for she hastily withdrew, and did not reappear.

"Good gracious!" thought Varberg to himself; "who would ever have suspected her of a moonlight reverie?"

This discovery, however, made him very happy for the moment, and he concluded that after such a day's experience it was in no way humiliating to pay the flesh its due, and go to bed.

CHAPTER IV.

From Wartburg to Leipsic.

VARBERG rose late the next morning, and as he went down to breakfast he heard Miss Copley inquiring of the clerk about the departure of the next train. He had just time to devour a couple of eggs, and to scald his mouth with the coffee, but he had in return the satisfaction of relieving the ladies of their bundles, and of conducting them to the not very comfortable railroad car. In fact the best thing about the German railroads is their safety and the magnificent beards of the officials; but in the point of comfort they are but a slight improvement on the old-fashioned stage-coaches. Miss Bailey began to talk very fast to the conductor in English, at which the Teuton smiled complacently, and turned the lock in her face. Miss Copley, with a kind of humorous indulgence to the customs of the land, made herself comfortable as best she could, and before long was engaged in an airy little chat with her new friend. "How did you enjoy Weimar?" she asked as the train moved on. "I was there a few months ago. But it made me almost vow that I should never go sight-seeing again."

"Why so?"

"I don't wish to spoil your story. Give me first your impressions, and I shall give you mine afterwards."

He briefly recounted to her his experience in Weimar, and especially dwelt on the forlorn appearance of Schiller's rooms.

"To think that the great poet should die in that poor unpainted bed," he said. "And the mask of his face, taken after his death, lies there on the pillow with the calm lines of suffering still legible in its features. I almost shivered to see it."

"You didn't experience a holy shudder, did you?"

"I don't know if I should give it just that name."

"Well, I am glad you didn't. I went to Weimar with a cousin who has now returned to America. He suffered with a holy shudder in Schiller's house, although I am confident that he had never read a word of what Schiller has written."

"How do you know? You appear to be a confirmed skeptic."

"I will give you my reasons. If any one is grandiloquent it is in my nature to question the genuineness of his emotions. As for my cousin, I soon found an occasion to put him to the test. He was in rapture at the idea of sitting at the desk on which 'Wallenstein' had been written. I began to talk about 'Wallenstein,' and called his daughter Catharina, although I was well aware that her name was Thekla. Fred immediately swallowed the bait, and commenced to declaim about this Catharina. 'What a superb creature she is! What wonderful strength of passion,' etc.—all generalities which might in fact apply to any heroine of a drama."

He couldn't help laughing at the novelty of the experiment, and still he was not altogether pleased. She evidently observed this, and hastened to add an explanation.

"I am always disappointed with myself whenever I visit the scene of a great historical event or the place where a great man has lived and died. I never succeed in associating the event or the man with the place. Somehow or other my sentiments are always off duty, and I remain provokingly cold. I believe that I could have cried with Mark Twain at the grave of Adam; but as for Schiller and the more modern benefactors of the race, I have no tears to waste on them."

Varberg sat regarding her face attentively while she spoke. He secretly admitted the truth of what she said, and honored her sincerity, although her remarks did seem to imply a doubt as to his own candor. He would probably have undertaken to defend himself, if it had not just then occurred to him that he had been unpardonably rude in excluding the less attractive cousin from the conversation. He hastened to repair the wrong. "And what do *you* think, Miss Bailey?" he said, turning to the latter.

"I think that this landscape is perfectly beautiful," answered Miss Bailey, in her peculiarly emphatic manner. And soon they were all engaged in a lively discussion of the comparative merits of a German and an American summer. Miss Copley grew very animated in the defence of her native land, while Varberg and Miss Bailey, whose home recollections could not have been of a very cheerful character, upheld the superiority of Europe.

The landscape through which they were just travelling did seem to add an argument in favor of the Teutons. On both sides of the road the vine-clad hills shone with the fresh tints of summer; the sunlight fell in brilliant profusion upon the glimmering rocks, and soft patches of shadow rested with the lightness of a noonday reverie upon the green banks of the Saale. About midway between the cities Naumburg and Weissenfels they observed the picturesque ruins of the old castles Rudolfsburg and Saaleck, whose shattered watch-towers stand like hoary Titans guarding the entrance to the valley.

"What untold tragedies, what idyls and romances have been enacted within those walls," said Varberg, pointing to the ruin.

"I wonder what house in New England that is twenty years old has not been the stage of similar tragedies and romances," answered Miss Ruth.

"Yes; if you would call a drunken shoemaker, who ruins his family, a romantic character, or a Wall Street speculator, who kills himself when he has lost his last stake."

"I can hardly comprehend," retorted she, with some little show of patriotic zeal, "why a drunken baron should be any more romantic than a drunken shoemaker; and you will no doubt admit that drunkenness was even more prevalent among your feudal heroes than among the Massachusetts shoemakers."

"I once knew a man out in Indiana," remarked Miss Bailey, "who killed himself drinking, and then killed all his family too."

"I am glad he was sensible enough to kill himself first," said her cousin dryly.

"Well, Ruth, I know you understand what I mean," cried Miss Bailey in a high-pitched staccato. "I somehow always get hold of the story by the wrong end, but if you only wouldn't be so particular—"

"Never mind, Dearie," interrupted the other. "You know you are the most charming person to tease; and," added she in a humorously tender tone, "you wouldn't begrudge me that pleasure, Dearie, would you?"

The train stopped at Weissenfels, and the melodious clocks of the station announced with six measured strokes the arrival. Half a dozen gorgeously uniformed officials began to run back and forth between the cars and the telegraph offices, stopping every minute or two to exchange a military salute. A young man with a fine sword at his side, a broad scarlet collar on his coat, and spectacles on his nose, strutted up and down on the pavement in front of the window of our travellers.

"Of what rank would you take that man to be?" said Varberg to Miss Bailey.

"I should suppose he was a colonel, or something of the sort," answered the lady.

"He is a clerk in the railroad office."

"How do you know?"

"I know it by the uniform. I travelled with a German professor from Kiel to Hanover, and had him instruct me in regard to many features of Prussian rule."

"I don't think the young man would do for

a ticket agent on the Boston and Albany road," observed Miss Ruth. " He has evidently sufficient conceit, but I doubt if he has the faculty of snubbing the public with that grand air which is so peculiar to our railroad men."

At Corbetha they changed cars, and the train now hastened on through a fertile, rather monotonous plain, where the stiff, tall poplars and the wide-spreading blades of the windmills keep up a silent contest for the sole proprietorship of the horizon. Friendly little villages cluster with their turf-thatched roofs about the oak-sheltered Gothic spire, and then disperse with a kind of youthful waywardness, strangely out of keeping with their general sombreness of aspect. In some instances the churches, with their square towers and their huge black roofs, seem to blend into a friendly harmony with their lowly surroundings; but at times they lord it over them, and the humble whitewashed cottages look as if they were crouching in the dust at the feet of their magnificent neighbors. As Ruth remarked, it reminded her of a poor family that had inherited a silver table service, but couldn't with their best will keep up the style which such an article required, nor could they make up their minds to part with it; and consequently everything else in the house looked poorer than it really was, only because the silver overshadowed it with its splendor.

"What would you do yourself in such a case, Miss Copley?" asked Varberg—"I mean if you were a member of such a family."

"I would go and sell the table service, and make myself comfortable with the money," answered she.

"And what would you do, Miss Bailey?"

"I would give it to some poor person."

"Who would be worse off with it than you had been yourself," cried Ruth, laughing. "Yes, I am sure that would be wise. But what would you do with it, Mr. Varberg?"

"I should keep it," said Olaf gravely.

Early in the afternoon the train reached Leipsic, and Olaf Varberg parted from his friends, after having helped them into a carriage, and having received a cordial invitation to call. As he rode home to his lodgings in the new part of the city, he reviewed in his mind the strange events of these two days. Mingled feelings of enchantment and displeasure were struggling in his bosom. No sooner was Ruth out of sight than he tried mercilessly to analyze her, in the hope of accounting for the fascination which her mere presence had exercised over him, or perhaps rather to prove to himself that his admiration was altogether foolish and irrational.

"She would make an admirable character for a story," he thought to himself; "some truly capital traits. But she has no two things in common with me; she ridicules the things which I love, and has no more appreciation of the romantic than a bat. The idea of my falling in love with such a woman"; and he laughed to himself at the absurdity of the thing. "No, it is a mere literary interest I take in her—a mere æsthetic regard."

"A mere æsthetic regard," he repeated as he entered his neatly furnished parlor. The phrase appeared striking to him, and he kept murmuring it, half absently, while he promenaded up and down the floor. And the longer he walked the more satisfied he grew that it was merely in his capacity of author that he loved Ruth, and that Olaf Varberg the man felt no particular interest in her.

"And then, had I better commence the story at once?" he asked himself; which question led to a brief dispute between Varberg the author and Varberg the man in regard to what course the latter ought to pursue toward the object of the former's love. It was finally agreed that Varberg the man should humor the wishes of his literary brother, and accept Miss Copley's invitation to continue the acquaintance.

Having settled this important business, our Norseman made a rather elaborate toilet, and repaired to the hotel where he was in the habit of taking his dinner. On the way he met his friend, Baron von Weisskopf, who embraced him in German fashion and kissed his cheeks, much to the disgust of the American part of his nature.

"Mein lieber Doctor," cried the Baron (all his German friends called him doctor), "I have sought you in all imaginable places for the last week, but have been unable to find you. I thought you might possibly be both dead and buried."

"Weeds do not perish so easily," replied Varberg.

"Ah, you are too modest, my excellent friend," cried Weisskopf gaily. "But by the way, where are you going?"

"I am going to my hotel, and should be happy to have you come and dine with me."

"With the greatest pleasure."

Arm in arm they wandered down the promenade, while the Baron related the last week's news from the student world, consisting chiefly of duels that had just taken place, and duels that were yet in prospect.

Baron Max von Weisskopf was a man of about six feet, stoutly built, and of a magnificient physique. His features were rather large and handsome, but they were marred by half a dozen scars which his full blonde beard but partly concealed. His brown hair was cut close to his head, and his eyes were protruding and had a glassy look. He had the neck of a bull, and the voice of a lion; his laugh was loud, and sounded like the clashing of two brazen pans. He was Varberg's senior by several years, but had taken a great fancy to him on their first meeting at a students' festival. As for the Norseman, he had never entertained any cordial regard for his noisy friend, but his literary zeal had induced him to continue the friendly relation. Weisskopf was an original character, he thought, and was especially useful in initiating him into the mysteries of German student life.

As consenior of one of the largest *chores*,* and a renowned swordsman, the Baron had, of course, free access everywhere, and it cost him but a word to gain for his friend the same privileges. His twenty-eight duels had covered him with honor and with "noble scars," which latter he took a special pride in displaying, whenever the Rhine wine had made him more than usually animated.

In the hotel a very abundant dinner was ordered, and Weisskopf ate and drank like a Hercules. Varberg was not in a mood to talk, and so he contented himself with keeping the Baron's glass constantly filled, and the Baron did his best to keep him steadily busy. When the

---

* *Chores* and *Burschenschaften* are the names of two kinds of students' societies, or rather organizations, at the German universities.

meal was at an end it was already late in the afternoon, and as they had nothing else to do they decided to pay a visit to Auerbach's "Keller." Through the entrance on Grimmaische Strasse they descended into the famous old vault, and Weisskopf ordered a couple of Johannisbergers, stole a kiss from a pretty waiting-maid who appeared in the door for a moment, and then conducted his friend into those queer old apartments, hallowed by a thousand memories dear to the German heart. They took their seats at one of the small tables, and glanced over the journals, until the waiter brought the long-necked bottles in a cooler. A kind of musty, mediæval smell filled the atmosphere of the vault, and the light fell in, like a dim, dusty current, through that narrow slit of window which was not covered by the pavement of the street. Varberg lighted a cigar, and handed his case to his companion.

"Well, lieber Doctor," said the latter, filling the glasses, "what do you think of our German ladies?"

"I like our American ones better," replied Varberg, to whose mind Ruth was for the time being the representative of American young ladyhood. Moreover he had quite forgotten his late enthusiasm for the Teuton maidens as long as he had imagined her a romantic Margaret.

"But you have hardly had an opportunity to judge yet," remarked the Baron. "Allow me some time or other to introduce you to my friend the actress, Fräulein B——, and I will wager six Johannisbergers that within a week you will be converted."

Weisskopf stretched out his hand across the table, and Varberg shook it silently.

"When I was in Italy a couple of years ago," continued the Teuton, whose flushed face was beginning to show the effect of the wine, "I was as full of prejudices as you are. But one day I took it into my head to learn the language of the country, and for that purpose I picked up an acquaintance with a young native woman, a truly magnificent creature, who had big black eyes—as big as that" (and the speaker put his thumbs and his first fingers together, and showed an opening about the size of a tea-cup). "Truly, I don't exaggerate. She had a voice like a nightingale, and a mouth—well, you can imagine the mouth—truly superb. One evening we met on the strand in the bay of Naples; I laid my hand about her waist, I kissed her lips, etc., and before we knew it, we were engaged."

"Do you mean to say," exclaimed Varberg, "that you proposed to her for the purpose of learning Italian?"

"Well, call it what you please," said the Baron, laughing heartily. "I certainly did learn the most exquisitely tender phrases which the Italian or any other language is capable of. And the amusing part of it was that I shocked two ladies whom I had never seen before by unconsciously addressing them with the most endearing names. In fact I discovered that I had, so to speak, skimmed the cream of the language, and that my vocabulary consisted merely of those delicately flushed words and phrases which sounded so ravishingly on Marietta's lips, and which, when I addressed them to her in return, she listened to with a delight as if she heard them for the first time in her life."

"I suppose you would advise me on the same principle to make love to some German maiden, as the most profitable mode of pursuing my philological studies."

"By all means, dear friend," and again the Baron laughed immoderately. "I shall be most happy to further your noble aim; and in return I shall expect of you that you introduce me to some of your American beauties here in the city, that I may have an opportunity of perfecting myself in English."

Varberg took it all for a pleasant joke, and laughed in a way which might have been interpreted as assent or as refusal. He pledged his friend in a sparkling glass, and tried to change the subject. But Weisskopf was not to be prevailed upon.

"At the next *Seminar** I shall know whether you have followed my advice," roared he. "Ah, what a delicious situation! To have you grave and proper American suddenly surprise our worthy Professor with some perfumed phrase of tenderest endearment."

Love stories, says Goethe, have this in

---

* *Seminar* is a half-private meeting of students and professors, and is usually devoted to the discussion of some particular linguistic or scientific topic.

common with ghost-stories: when one has told his experience the listeners are invariably infected with a similar desire to relate theirs. Weisskopf had roamed about considerably, and wherever he came it was as natural for him to engage himself as to hire his board and lodgings. With an amiable nonchalance he flitted from adventure to adventure, and touched upon numerous incidents, not always of a strictly moral character, with an airy cheerfulness which went far to remove Varberg's scruples, and at last made him look upon himself as an unpardonable prude for ever having disapproved of him. Thus the end of it was that Olaf, from a half-confessed desire to establish himself in his friend's respect, began to relate his early romance with the Colonel's daughter in Norway, but as he progressed he became more disagreeably aware of its poverty in comparison with the Baron's glowing descriptions, and in order to make up for its lack of incident he unconsciously raised Thora to the dignity of a sort of Northern sea-princess, while he himself assumed the character of an heroic, self-sacrificing lover. Indeed, that part of his life seemed so infinitely remote, as if he had read of it a long time ago in some Oriental fairy tale; he treated himself altogether impersonally, and vaguely believed that Thora was all that his fancy made her. About Wartburg and Ruth he said not a word.

"But my dearest Doctor," cried Weisskopf, as the other had finished, "what an egregious ass you must have been—I mean, of course, in your younger years—to let such a chance slip through your fingers!"

Varberg felt the force of the remark, and could think of nothing to offer as an excuse. He did seem to have acted stupidly, and he felt as guilty as if he had committed a dishonorable act. Strange to say, it is often more humiliating to be outdone by our friends in folly than to be excelled by them in wisdom. The evening was already far advanced, and at Olaf's suggestion they rose to go. The waiter came to collect the money; Weisskopf pulled out his purse, and with a half-provoked air began to hunt for some thaler bills which he didn't find.

"Ah, lieber Doctor," he exclaimed, "I forgot to supply my purse as I passed my banker to-day. You will no doubt help me out of my embarrassment."

Varberg immediately handed him a ten-thaler note, and Weisskopf paid the waiter, and as a matter of course put the remaining amount into his own pocket-book. But he did it with an air which made Varberg dimly feel as if he ought to be grateful to him for condescending to accept the favor.

They separated on the Augustus-Platz, and Varberg took a carriage and drove home. Without lighting the gas, he flung himself into the corner of the sofa, and a train of confused thoughts whirled through his head. He thought of Ruth, and he thought of Weisskopf, and the one appeared to him like the good angel, and the other as the evil demon of his life. A blush of shame stole to his face, as he compared the noble aspirations of the morning with the imbecile boasts of the night.

"*I* introduce *him* to Ruth!" he cried. "Nay, rather shall our swords clash and my bloody corpse shall bar him the entrance."

Olaf Varberg was fond of tall phrases, especially when talking with himself.

CHAPTER V.

In Rosenthal.

IN one of the most fashionable streets of Leipsic there is a tall and gloomily comfortable mansion which has become a kind of traditional resort for Americans. Our people do not take kindly to tradition when at home, but for this very reason they like to flirt with it abroad, and are even willing to put up with a good deal of personal discomfort for the mere pleasure of being able to write to their friends beyond the sea, " From my windows I look out upon the mouldering arches of a ruined Capuchin convent"; or, " I write this sitting on a spot which is said to be haunted by the august shade of the Emperor Barbarossa." And the honest people of Germany, who have discovered this weakness in their visitors, are not unlikely to manufacture legends for the occasion in order thereby to invest their humble abodes with that romantic charm which seldom fails to act as a bait to travellers: and it is needless to add that they enhance their prices accordingly. Between Göttingen and the Harz there is hardly a forest or a mountain which does not lay claim to some association with Barbarossa's ghost, and in Eisenach every other house has been the scene of some remarkable incident in the lives of Luther, the Minnesingers, or Sebastian Bach. In Leipsic, square marble tablets with the inscription, "Hier ward geboren," etc., or, "Hier starb," adorn the houses where great men have lived, or died, and Varberg had, naturally enough, made the round of these houses before he condescended to resort to the new and unhistorical part of the city. Unfortunately they were all occupied, and for want of anything better he had selected a mansion which had been hit by a cannon ball in the last battle of Leipsic, and which from that day bore the inscription, "Behüte Gott dieses Haus." (God protect this house.)

Ruth had been more fortunate in the choice of her dwelling. As already observed, it was situated in one of the most fashionable streets, and was a kind of cross between the old and the new city. On one side it bordered on the lazily-flowing Pleisse, which had once, if the story be true, flowed red with the mingled blood of brave French and German hearts; a round-arched vault, pleasantly suggestive of cloisters and mediæval life, led from the street into a paved court, three sides of which were enclosed by high walls, while the fourth left the view free toward a half rural oasis, with low-roofed cottages and little green garden patches.

Ruth had been living here for about a year, with her aunt and cousin, at the time when Varberg made her acquaintance. She was the only daughter of a retired Boston merchant, and had never been out of Massachusetts until she went abroad. At the age of five she had lost her mother, and her father, who was a hardworking man and had but little time to devote to his child, had given her in charge of a widowed aunt, Mrs. Elder, the mother of the cousin Fred whose enthusiasm for Schiller Ruth had so pitilessly ridiculed. Old Mr. Copley had since the death of his wife almost shunned the society of ladies, and consequently his daughter had, from her earliest childhood, been thrown largely into the company of men who had always flattered her and humored her wishes. Her aunt, who was a weak and gentle woman, soon became aware of the intellectual superiority of her ward, and her conduct toward her showed the latter that she tacitly recognized this superiority. Thus Ruth early acquired a certain independence of manner and a fearlessness in expressing her opinions which by the less charitable of her own sex were interpreted as wilfulness and *hauteur*. Nevertheless, as she grew up to young ladyhood, she was eagerly sought in society, and those whom she deigned to admit into her confidence felt honored by her friendship, and became ardently attached to her. There was something in her manner which put an end to all criticism; whatever she did, the fact that it was she who did it, sanctioned it and made it proper.

It was about a week since the young ladies had returned from Wartburg. Ruth was sitting at the piano playing snatches of various airs, and now and then giving an impatient toss of her head, as she opened and again threw away one piece of music after the other.

"Schumann was a nursery hero," she said, turning about on the stool. "I can't imagine how Clara Shumann could take it into her head to marry him. If I had been she, I would rather have married old W——."

W—— was an old Leipsic music teacher, of whom it is said that he forswore composing because Clara Schumann refused his love.

"And why do you play him then, my dear?" said Mrs. Elder, who was seated on the sofa doing some sort of worsted work.

"I have to do a great many things which I disapprove of, aunt," replied Ruth, wheeling again round to the piano. "There is a strange sort of fascination about him which I can't resist, although his capriciousness provokes me the more for every measure I play."

"Ah, there he is coming," ejaculated Miss Bailey, who had in the meanwhile been looking out of the window.

"Who is coming, Dearie?" asked the aunt

"Our Wartburg friend."

Miss Bailey's real name was Sarah; but once

when she had been very sick, and had not been expected to live, the family had got into the habit of calling her Dearie, and this name she had ever since retained. When Ruth wanted to tease her she called her Sallie, which name, for some reason or other, was exceedingly repugnant to its owner; in fact Ruth, who was not loth to employ stratagem for the accomplishment of her wishes, could induce her cousin to do anything in the world for her by the promise that she would never more call her Sallie.

No sooner had Miss Bailey announced that the Wartburg friend was coming than Ruth rose from the piano, and began to busy herself about the room, clearing away books and work-baskets from the table, and putting things into order.

There was a knock at the door. Mrs. Elder responded with a gentle "Come in," and Varberg entered. He greeted the ladies, and was introduced to Mrs. Elder.

"Why, you speak English!" exclaimed she. "I understood that you were a German, or something of that sort."

Ruth sent her aunt a quick, disapproving

glance, and Mrs. Elder determined that she would say nothing more.

"No, I am not a German," replied Varberg, as he suffered himself to be led to a seat. "I have no wish to change my nationality."

"We feared that you had quite forgotten us, Mr. Varberg," said Ruth. "You have not been in haste to find out where we lived."

Olaf murmured some kind of commonplace excuse, and the conversation was turned on some fresh topic.

"I am glad you are not a German," remarked Mrs. Elder, who had in the meanwhile forgotten her resolution. "The Germans are very unintelligent people. They eat with their knives, and the gentlemen always supply themselves first at the table, and leave the ladies to take care of themselves."

"I should hardly ascribe that to lack of intelligence," replied Varberg. "I think I should rather call it rudeness, or lack of good breeding."

"I should call it simply immoral," said Ruth, with a humorous sparkle in her eye, which left the listener in doubt whether she was jesting or really in earnest.

"The term is a matter of indifference to me," answered he, "if the fact still remains. But I must say that I have not invariably found the Germans impolite."

"My chief objection to the Teuton males," observed Ruth laughing, "is that they eat sourkrout and strong cheese and smoke bad tobacco. And the ladies I disapprove of because they look dowdyish."

Varberg was once more about to undertake the defence of the Teutons, when it occurred to him that the weather was beautiful, and that the time would be most favorable for a walk through Rosenthal. He ventured to make a proposition to that effect, and the ladies willingly assented. While they withdrew to the next room to put on their things he again addressed himself to Mrs. Elder, and had an opportunity of becoming better acquainted with that estimable matron. Mrs. Elder was a plump old lady, with a kind, benevolent face of an enviably clear complexion; her white hair fell smoothly over her low forehead, and her mild blue eyes and her soft voice gave one the impression of a patient, forbearing indolence. There was not the remotest suggestion of anything aggressive about Mrs. Elder's whole person; she seemed to be gentleness and forbearance personified. As soon as she had learned a few facts relating to the visitor's early life, she began to tell him what a prodigy Ruth had been from the time she was old enough to talk; and Varberg listened eagerly, and was quite ready to believe that his heroine possessed even far greater excellences than the old lady would have thought of claiming for her.

"I remember once when she was four years old," said Mrs. Elder, "her mother and I were sitting in the parlor, and we were talking about some person who was in the habit of coming to the house quite frequently. I was about to say something not exactly favorable about this person, but my sister-in-law pointed to Ruth, who was sitting in a corner playing with her dolls, and said, 'Little pitchers have ears.' 'Yes, and legs too,' replied Ruth, picked up her dolls, and marched out of the room. Now, don't you think that was a remarkable answer for a child four years old?"

Varberg did own that the repartee was excellent, and the aunt proceeded to give fresh instances of her niece's precocity, and the young man continued to listen with the same unflagging interest and devotion. At length the ladies returned, but Miss Bailey suddenly declared that she had a headache, and that she could not go. Ruth said it was only imagination, and sprinkled her with eau-de-cologne, but Miss Bailey was not to be prevailed upon. So Ruth and Varberg started alone.

It had rained early in the day; the air was pure and summer-like, and the soil still exhaled that damp earthy smell which after a shower always affects one's senses so agreeably. Ruth was in excellent humor, and made her half sarcastic little remarks upon everybody that passed. But as they entered Rosenthal, the park of Leipsic, the promenaders became too numerous, and she was not a little puzzled to make a judicious choice among so many tempting subjects for her satire.

Rosenthal must have been named on the *lucus a non lucendo* principle, for it is neither a valley (*Thal*) nor are there roses in it. It is on the contrary a large and perfectly level plain, the outskirts of which are overgrown with maple and beech forest, while the middle part seems hardly yet to have been reclaimed from its natural state of moor and pasture land. But the principal feature of the park, speaking from a German point of view, is the large and excellent restaurant, with its rudely frescoed pavilions, its fragrant coffee, and its old-world look of cheer and comfort. Our wanderers, however, did not on this occasion yield to the temptation of the restaurant, but wended their way onward beneath the shady crowns of the full-leafed beeches. Ruth assumed to-day, as ever, a patronizing attitude toward the natives; and Varberg, who seldom of his own accord discovered the humorous side of anything—abstract or concrete—was soon allured into a heartier participation in her merriment, and even astonished himself by little speeches which a month ago he would have condemned as flippant and irreverent, had they been uttered by anybody but himself. As they entered a little side path, at the end of which a green arbor invited to rest, Ruth discovered a voluminous Leipsicker who, with half-open eyes and a fat, lazy expression in his countenance, lay outstretched on a bench at the roadside; half a dozen ruddy-cheeked and sleepy-looking children, who appeared to be all of about the same age, played in a sort of meek fashion about him on the grass, while occasional grunts broke from the worthy parent's throat, indicating his parental watchfulness and supervision.

"Behold a typical Saxon," said Varberg.

"I should rather say a typical Leipsicker," remarked Ruth.

"How would you define, or what place in the animal kingdom would you assign to the native Leipsicker?"

"If I had to write an essay about him, I think I should have to commence in this way: The native Leipsicker is an amphibium. His blood is lukewarm, and he breathes by means of lungs, but a close observer will detect an indication of gills on the nether side of the jaws. His favorite element is lager beer; but but on a warm day the male may be seen sunning himself on the banks of Rosenthal, etc."

There is always mystery enough about a forest arbor to gently attune two hearts into mutual sympathy. Varberg had enjoyed her merry sarcasms; he had laughed at the drollness of her criticisms, and he had even succeeded beyond his expectation in entering into her mood. Nevertheless this was not his way of looking upon life; she saw only the grotesque and ludicrous, while his chief pleasure was to note the quaint and the picturesque, to detect the fleeting shades and *nuances* of color, and to catch characteristic glimpses of the land and the people among whom he was living. Unhappily they were both a little exclusive, and their point of view one-sided. Had Olaf possessed her quick sense of humor, or had she been gifted with his keen sight for the picturesque, they would both have been more ideal companions, and would perhaps have reaped greater profit from their German sojourn than they did. As it was, their views and purposes came into constant collision, and there was a Wartburg or a forest arbor, or some equally romantic neighborhood needed to breathe upon some hidden chord in her bosom so as to make it vibrate in conscious sympathy with him. There was to him a delicious sense of security in being thus shut out from all the obtrusive world, and being, if but for moment, alone in this secluded forest haunt with one so young and so wondrously fair. A stray glint of sunshine fell through the leaves and hung trembling above her head, and he now noticed for the first time that she had on her hat a small bird of paradise which, with open bill, seemed to pursue a glittering little bug, attached to a straw at half an inch's distance.

"She certainly has fancy," he thought, "and what is more, she has the courage to trust in the verdict of her own taste."

"Tell me, Mr. Varberg," said Ruth abruptly, piercing a maple leaf and balancing it on the end of her parasol; "how did you ever conceive the idea of writing a book?"

"I was not aware that I had ever claimed in your presence the character of an author."

"Oh, yes, you have," and she looked up archly. "It is of no use to try to disguise yourself before me. I had read your book some time before I saw you, and I discovered at Wartburg who you were, even before you gave me your name."

"You astonish me, Miss Copley. However, in regard to your question, it is very difficult to say when or how any one conceives the idea of writing a book. I wrote my first book when I was ten years old; only it was never printed. Since then I have assumed to myself the character of an author, and even if my tales and poems were never printed, and no one else was willing to recognize me in my assumed capacity, it would still be as natural to me to write as it would be to eat and to sleep, and I should until the day of my death look upon myself as an author."

"How strange," she murmured absently, and then suddenly straightening herself up, she added in a livelier tone, "Have you the patience to listen to a little secret of mine which I feel inclined to confide to you?"

"I am all attention."

"Very well then. You would hardly believe it, but I too once wrote a story. I wrote it, not because I felt it an inward necessity to write, but because I thought it would be nice to see something of my own in print. And then, you know, most people think, when they have read a novel, that they might just as well have written it themselves; and with young girls at least I know it is a very natural impulse to test their capacity at once, and to try in some way or other to imitate what they read."

"And may I ask what was the fate of your book?"

"Wait a little. I have not got to that point yet. I plotted the story, and I thought at the time that it was quite as good as a hundred I had read. But when I commenced to write it, innumerable difficulties presented themselves; and what especially puzzled me was that my characters would invariably get talking on some profound topic which I myself knew nothing about. And then, you see, I would always come to a sudden stop. At last I gave it up in despair, and owned that I was not born an authoress. But since that time I have had a sincere respect for those who possessed the gift which was denied me."

"I can hardly take the compliment to myself, Miss Copley," replied Varberg, "since my incipient authorship has as yet proved nothing. It may be all assumption on my part, but," he added after a pause, "it will at least take a lifetime to convince me of it."

"I shall not flatter you," she said laughing;

"although I have a tempting opportunity to do so." And both arose and turned into a narrow path leading to an oak which has lately been planted in commemoration of the German victories over France. Ruth began to talk about America, and mentioned some friends of hers in Boston whose acquaintance she hoped Varberg would make when he should return to the city of the Puritans. Varberg also mentioned some friend of his, and wondered that she had never heard of him.

"He is a very good—in fact, an excellent young man," he said.

"Oh, I am sure I should dislike him," answered she emphatically. "I always dislike excellent young men."

"I am afraid I don't understand you."

"No; I am afraid you do not. When anybody tells me that a young man is good or excellent, I always infer that he is stupid. For if he wasn't, people would think of something else to say about him. And stupid men I have no patience with."

"And do you apply the same test to ladies?"

"Well, it isn't so unpardonable in ladies to

be stupid. In fact, they are in a way shut out from the great interests of mankind. They move in an old, steady-going routine, and if they have no great aims or aspirations to spur them on, they can hardly escape being dull and commonplace. And you have, no doubt, yourself noticed how uncharitable men are toward those very women who have the courage to rise a little above what is called their proper sphere of life. What a man demands of a woman is innocence and stupidity."

Varberg tacitly admitted the justice of her accusation, and she suspected from his silence that he agreed with her.

"To authors," he said after a pause, "these women whom you call dull and commonplace are often as interesting as those who rise above their sphere."

"How so, pray? You speak in riddles."

"I am afraid I shall give you a wrong impression if I attempt to explain what I mean. However, since I have said A, I must say B also.* As a reporter or a newspaper correspondent is apt to look upon the world as a conglomerate of

* A Norwegian proverb.

items, so an author is in danger of regarding it as a confused heap of plots, which it is for him to discover, to disentangle, and to arrange into a symmetrical work of art. If he sees joy or suffering, happy or unhappy events, he may merely estimate their literary value, and wonder how they would look in print; and the most dangerous part of it is that, like a dissecting surgeon, he may soon lose his sympathy and fellow-feeling for his brethren. He rejoices in a fine burst of despair, keenly relishes a deep and exalted grief, and derives an intense enjoyment from every pure and vigorous expression of emotion which may come in his way."

He would have continued his harangue, but here his fair companion stopped, as if in surprise, and looked him wistfully in the eye.

"What horrid people authors must be!" she exclaimed. "I take back every word I have said about my loyalty and respect for them."

"Wait until I have finished. Mind, I don't say that authors are as I have described them. I have merely said that they are in danger of becoming so. Thus, as long as your commonplace ladies are capable of a pure, human emotion, they are objects of interest to an author. He often imagines himself standing upon a high pedestal, like a Simon Stylites, and he sees the noisy whirl of life eddying about his pillar, but he is not moved. Life becomes a pageantry to him in a more specific sense. Pure, typical features delight him, and men and women assume in their relation to him merely the character of good or bad figures for a story. But remember, this is merely an imaginary picture. If authors were not human enough to fall in love, it would be a real one. But unhappily, from their exalted station, they are very likely to discover some maidenly face, typical or not; a wild longing seizes them; they madly plunge down into the whirlpool in pursuit of this maiden, and if they find her, are henceforth content to read nothing but the tender mystery of her heart, and to see nothing but that little domestic idyl which soon nestles about them."

"Your picture is certainly a striking one. I never looked upon it in that way before. But you say 'unhappily'; do you then think that it is a misfortune to be capable of love?"

"I do not know," he murmured sadly. Their

eyes met in a quick glance. "I only wish that I was myself less capable of it."

A deep blush stole over her cheeks, and she unconsciously hastened her steps. In a few minutes they reached the memorial oak, which was hedged in by an open iron fence. The small enclosure within was laid out into flower beds, in which grew pansies, lilies, and tulips in many-colored profusion.

"What a beautiful pansy!" Ruth exclaimed, pointing with her hand through the iron bars. "I never saw a larger one."

No sooner had she uttered the words than he bounded over the fence, picked the flower, and handed it to her.

"But, Mr. Varberg, what are you doing?" she cried in a frightened voice. "Don't you know that it is forbidden to pick those flowers? If the police saw you, they would arrest you."

"What do I care for the police?" said he, as he stood again at her side. "Not all the police in the German empire could prevent me from taking a flower if—if—you wanted it," he added in a precipitous flutter. She took the pansy, and they moved on. A strange recklessness had come over him; in one moment he felt hot and flushed, and in the next he shivered. He was afraid of speaking lest he should betray his agitation.

"Do not hold the flower in your left hand, Miss Copley," he said at last, when the silence became too oppressive. "It will wither. You are aware that there is an old superstition about it, and you know I claim to be superstitious."

"It will die and become a ghost," answered Ruth musingly, and looking at the flower. "You remember what you told me about the elf maidens. And the flower-ghost will haunt you and tread an airy dance about you in the moonlight. Ah, you see I have profited by your instruction. It is strange," she added after a pause, "all your legendary beings show a predilection for men. One seldom hears of their molesting women."

He was not in the mood for legends to-day, and the topic was soon dropped. On their way back to the city they met the Baron von Weisskopf, and as he had the rudeness to stop and talk to Varberg, the latter had hardly any choice but to introduce him; but he did it with a fierce scowl on his brow and in an indifferent voice, which must have puzzled his friend exceedingly.

"Aha," said the Baron to himself, as he turned to the restaurant's pavilion to order his coffee with *curaçao*, "he is studying the American tongue for the present. That accounts for it."

"What a magnificent neck he had!" observed Ruth to her companion.

"Yes, his neck is his most prominent feature," answered Varberg.

Under the old archway of the house where she lived they parted.

"You will come and see us very often now, won't you?" said she, as she reached him her hand and vanished through the door.

With an airily uncertain tread, and the absurdest fancies hovering through his brain, Varberg reached his own dwelling. Now he hummed a snatch of a song, now he thrust his hands into his pocket, and began to march distractedly up and down the floor; now again he wondered what he had thought about the minute before, paused suddenly in his walk, and placed his finger meditatively on his nose.

"Good heavens!" cried he aloud. "What can be the matter with me? I never felt so in my life before."

In order to find something to occupy his thought, he opened his writing desk and began to glance over some old letters and poems. And from out of the old verses his former self seemed to stare upon him like an indignant ghost, upbraiding him for having disturbed its peace. It appeared a perfect mystery to Varberg that he had ever been as those poems showed him to have been, and still he distinctly remembered the occasion; it was only a few months since they had been written.

"What wretched stuff!" he exclaimed at last. And he went to the window, tore the poems to small pieces, and scattered the fragments on the wind. Like a swarm of frightened butterflies they rose and fell in the air, whirled giddily around and flew out over the roofs of the city. Olaf even wondered if one of them might not reach Ruth's window, and he was about to construct a little romance out of it, when it struck him that it was a very trite and threadbare sentiment.

CHAPTER VI.

Brother Jonathan's Ball.

DURING the following four weeks there was hardly a day in which Ruth and Varberg did not meet. If he stayed away for a couple of days, she accused him of being unneighborly, and he was too conscientious to plead business or accidental obstacles, when all the time he felt that no business in the world would have had the power to call him away from her side. But the truth was, he was living in a state of perpetual struggle with himself; his life seemed but one long-continued contradiction. And at certain periods, fresh scruples would beset him, and strange misgivings would fill his heart. Was it merely an æsthetic regard he felt for Ruth? Was it merely the artist in him who admired and loved her? and was it only as the possible heroine of a future story that he felt his heart warming toward her and his thoughts circling about her in unending and ever-narrowing spheres? And suppose that his attitude toward her was merely that of a disinterested observer: was it then the part of an upright and honorable man to steal thus occultly, under the cover of friendship, into a young girl's heart, only to explore its hidden workings, and then expose it ruthlessly to the stare of an unsympathetic multitude? He might try to persuade himself as much as he pleased, that he did it for the benefit of art, which stands high above all the petty interests of the individual; the better part of his nature would still rebel against this kind of proceeding; and the result was that Varberg the man and Varberg the artist declared each other war, and never wearied of heaping upon each other the fiercest accusations. Varberg the artist however, gained an advantage which he persistently clung to; it was absurd, he said, to think that Ruth should return the tender regard which he professed to cherish for her. It was on her part simply a friendship—a mere Platonic relation. Probably the thought of love had never entered her head. Thus persuaded, our Norseman would again, in a tenderly melancholy mood, wend his way toward the house with the archway, and as he entered the bright and cosy little parlor, and his eyes again eagerly drank the ever-fresh delight of her presence, he seemed to himself a famished wanderer who falls down exhausted at the border of the oasis, content to feel, if not to taste, the gifts of its bounty. He would often sit for hours wondering at the perfection of outline in her bust and countenance, and admiring the grace and elastic harmony of their curves; there was something Juno-like in them, he thought. She was evidently not of Germanic origin; there was a classic repose in the poise of her head, and there was merely a more single and primitive costume needed to reveal in her the plastic grace of the Periclean age. But with all this you would detect in her glance, in the *ensemble* of her face, and perhaps in the very features which Varberg liked to call Greek, something which instantly excluded the possibility of an old-world birth; perhaps it was a certain unconsciousness of restraint, a wholesome (or as Varberg styled it, shocking) disrespect for tradition. At all events, her whole being breathed the ethereal loveliness of American womanhood.

There was something ineffably delicious in these silent reveries—a luxury of being, a *dolce far niente*, which was rendered the sweeter by the consciousness that it was shared by her. In such moments these lines of Keats would float dimly through his mind:

> Dark nor light
> The region; nor bright nor sombre wholly,
> But mingled up; a gleaming melancholy;
> A dusky empire and its diadems;
> One faint eternal eventide of gems.

Keats had been his first love among poets; it was while turning over the leaves of his solitary volume that he had caught the first glimpse of the golden ore of the English tongue, and delving deeper, he had been startled at the revelation of all its unceasing wonder and delight. In Keats he had also found a line which for its association with Ruth had become infinitely dear to him:

> Perhaps the self-same song that found a path
> Through the sad heart of Ruth when, sick for home,
> She stood in tears amid the alien corn.

To be sure he had never seen Ruth in tears, nor did he imagine that she was "sick for home," but nevertheless the chasteness, the sculpturesque purity of the verse could not but suggest her. Ruth's cheeks were like the fresh-fallen snow, not in tint, but because they looked as if they had never been touched, and her lips were as if they had never been kissed.

Ruth had soon discovered that her friend was a *dilettante* in music, and after some hesitation he had consented to come and play duets with her once a week. For a time he was quite enthusiastic in his devotion to the noble art, and even practised faithfully, but his fingers had lost their suppleness, and he could no longer perform those feats of manual dexterity which Liszt's and Van Bülow's arrangements require. By virtue of patient labor, however, and a good deal of forbearance on her part, he brought it so far that he could play the bass with tolerable accuracy (and he was artist enough to do it unobtrusively) while she managed the treble part with consummate skill. If he lost his place, she swiftly pointed to it with her finger; if he was a measure behind, she at once noticed it, and adapted herself to him; and if he missed a flat or a sharp, her finger was in an instant on the right key, and all the time her own part was rendered to perfection. Varberg enjoyed these musical evenings well enough, but he confessed to himself that he felt just a trifle humiliated at being corrected even by her, and that it was a relief to him when she gave him furlough and allowed him lazily to listen to her own improvisations.

Varberg had, without any special effort of his own, soon established himself in Mrs. Elder's favor. The old lady, although she would persist in Anglicizing his name into Warbeck and even Warble, seemed to entertain a very cordial regard for him. In her opinion it was a sad mistake that all the world had not been made to speak English; and it always remained a mystery to her how people could communicate with each other in any other tongue. Against the German she moreover cherished a kind of personal resentment; she did not dare say so, but nevertheless it remained a source of fresh wonder to her how even children could express themselves with fluency in such a harsh and barbarous language. It was amusing to see the puzzled frown on her face when the servant maid came in and addressed some greeting or question to her; and Ruth asserted that when she had nothing else to do she usually went shopping with her aunt, for the mere sport of seeing the latter's indignant stare at being confronted with the Teuton clerks, and her unabated surprise at finding the German the language of every store they entered. And on such occasions Mrs. Elder, when she had recovered from her first shock, would never cease to marvel at the vastness of her niece's attainments, although her indiscriminate linguistic taste awarded a similar verdict of intellectual superiority to Miss Bailey, whose German was only remarkable for its reckless defiance of gender and syntax.

It was in the last days of June that a wealthy American residing in Leipsic gathered the *élite* of the English-speaking population at his house, for what was informally called "a social hop." The secret was let out some days before the invitations came, and the pupils of the Conservatory were all in a flutter, and puzzled themselves with endless conjectures as to who were to be among the favored few. It was also rumored that some aristocratic German friends were to be there. Ruth, Varberg, and Miss Bailey each received a dainty little note requesting the honor of their presence, and they very naturally agreed to go together; Varberg of course reserved for himself the pleasure of procuring a carriage, and the ladies were in return to consider themselves as being under his special charge. At the appointed time he made his appearance in the usual unpicturesque attire of this century's cavaliers, and Mrs. Elder reported that the ladies would soon be ready; but as Varberg had sufficient experience in such matters to know that "soon" meant at least an hour, he made himself comfortable in the sofa corner, and resolved to be patient. Mrs. Elder first asked him whether people ate meat in his country (she had a dim impression that they fed on tallow candles), and having been satisfied on this point, gave an account of Dearie's experience as a pupil in a Leipsic school.

"It was a most excellent school," said the old lady. "They had Brussels carpets on the floors in the school-rooms—and you know carpets are not a common luxury in this country—and they had servants who waited upon the scholars and reached them their books and everything they wanted. But then the teacher asked Dearie what the capital of the United States was called, and Dearie said that it was Washington. 'Why, don't you know better?' said the teacher. 'It is New York.' Dearie of course couldn't stand that, and she came home crying, and since then she hasn't been there."

Varberg expressed his approval of Dearie's action, and Mrs. Elder again gave vent to her curiosity about the mode of life among the Norwegians, whom, in spite of his assertion to the contrary, she would persist in confounding with the Laplanders. Did they have railroads in Norway? didn't the ladies there wear sheepskin dresses for evening parties? and didn't the gentlemen in polite society kick the rafter in the ceiling when entering a room? If she had intended to banter him, Varberg would have received her questions as pleasantry, and answered accordingly; but the distressing part of it was that she evidently spoke in good faith, and even cited authorities for her opinions whenever he ventured to contradict her. She knew she had read it somewhere, she said.

In the meanwhile a richly perfumed breeze (which made the lamp flutter) and an ethereal silken rustle announced Ruth's arrival, and Varberg suddenly grew very unpatriotic, and refused to listen to Mrs. Elder's discourse about Norway. But Dearie was not yet ready, and Mrs. Elder was too much warmed up to drop the subject at so critical a moment. The young man grew more and more uneasy, then vexed, and at last came very near being impolite; but Ruth came to his rescue.

"I am very sorry to have kept you waiting so long, Mr. Varberg," said she.

"Never mind, dear," interposed Mrs. Elder. "We have had a very pleasant time indeed. Mr. Warbeck has been telling me about his country."

"Ah!" exclaimed Ruth with animation. "Do not let me interrupt you. I shall sit here quietly and listen. I am as much interested as aunt."

There was once more a great rustle of silk and freshly-ironed skirts while she gathered up her dress and let herself drop down on the piano stool. She crossed her hands in her lap, threw her head back, " Well, now you may begin. I am all attention."

Now Olaf had ever been proud of his country; but at this moment he hated it, because it seemed to remove him from her; he hated Mrs. Elder for reminding him of their dissimilarity, and he even hated that part of his own life which he had not shared with Ruth.

Never had Miss Bailey appeared lovelier in his eyes; and never had she been more welcome. He instinctively made the reflection that a ball attire does make even the plainest look attractive. Little did he heed the numerous injunctions from Mrs. Elder, about coming home in time, taking care that the ladies didn't drink ice-water when they were warm, etc. In an agreeably festive mood they descended the stairs, and in another minute the carriage door was slammed to, and they rolled away.

On the way Olaf engaged Ruth for the first waltz and the German and Miss Bailey for two quadrilles. As the former stepped from the carriage she had to put her hands on his shoulders and to make a little leap on to the sidewalk; and Miss Bailey did the same. In the hall on the second floor they parted, and the ladies went to the dressing-room ; and it was nearly half an hour before they returned. He in the meanwhile split his gloves from sheer distraction, and had to send a servant out to buy a fresh pair. Fortunately he reappeared within a few minutes. At length, when Varberg's patience was nearly gone, he felt a light pressure on his arm—it was Ruth.

We would fain gratify the reader with a description of what Ruth had on, but Varberg's journal, to which we are indebted for the plot of the present story, contains only the following passage which we prefer to quote in the original: "She was dressed in some sort of corn-colored stuff trimmed with black. She looked lovely as a fresh-opened rosebud. I don't think it was moire antique, nor was it calico."

The host and his daughter received the guests at the door. The former was a tall and thin man, with a Brother-Jonathan face and beard, and a huge diamond pin in his shirt-bosom ; the daughter was a pretty, fair-haired damsel, with an insignificant little face, and as Varberg maliciously remarked, she had, somehow or other, the air of having been bred in the oil regions. She evidently had taken this position at her father's side as a *souffleur*, for whenever a guest appeared she whispered his or her name, and the father made a feeble attempt at imitating it, but usually with indifferent success.

As Varberg, with Ruth on his arm, promenaded down the length of the large, well-lighted room, he heard some one exclaiming, as if quite involuntarily, "Donnerwetter? Wie wunderschön!" He turned his head indignantly, and to his astonishment saw his friend the Baron. Ruth dropped her eyes and blushed slightly.

"I wonder how *he* happened to come here," whispered she.

"He wishes for an opportunity to study English," replied Varberg with a dry laugh.

The musicians began to tune their instruments. The violins scraped and twanged with raising and falling inflection; the clarionets ran through some introductory trills; and the bass made a few asthmatic efforts of uncertain description; but suddenly, as by one common impulse, the tones rushed together into a warm embrace, wound their soft spirit arms around each other, and waved and rocked and floated onward on the delicious billowing rhythm of a Strauss waltz. One couple after another danced out on the floor. Varberg laid his arm about Ruth's waist; the exhilarating music seemed to have entered into his feet, and with the same softly rhythmical tread they whirled away now up, now down the room, now swiftly spinning around, now with a slow, deliberate step—in short, with all the delightful caprices of well-practised dancers.

"Are you tired?" he whispered. "Then only let me know."

"Never," answered she eagerly. "I never tire of a good waltz."

At length, as the music ceased, he led her, all aglow with pleasure, to the corner where Dearie was sitting. Dearie had been dancing with a Conservatory friend of hers, but he was from New York, and she from Indiana, and consequently they couldn't agree on any one kind of step. She was all out of patience with him, and had at last proposed to abandon the attempt. All this she told her cousin and her partner in a provoked voice and in her own emphatic way, until Varberg, who on account of her relation to Ruth had a kind of an elder-brotherly feeling toward her, claimed her partnership for the appointed quadrille. In an instant the Baron von Weisskopf skipped across the floor like a goat, and made a deep bow to Ruth; she arose, took his arm, and walked into a smaller room, where it appeared that a select set were dancing. Dearie was less interesting than usual this evening, and she refused to listen to Olaf's conversation. She merely asked incessantly, "Who is this?" and "Who is that?" and when he was unable to satisfy her curiosity she pouted and shook her ringlets impatiently. Later in the evening a still greater misfortune befell him. As the company was called out to supper he happened to be dancing a galop with the host's daughter, whose resources of conversation were deplorably scanty.

"Are you fond of dancing?" she said, as they sat down to the table. He gave some commonplace answer, and tried to introduce some fresh topic; and as he was in the midst of some glowing description, he heard his partner whispering to the servant—

"Pass the sauce for the turkey to the next table." And a minute later, in an undertone—

"Be sure that there is enough of the chicken salad. Don't bring in the large cake before I tell you."

This was truly discouraging; she had not heard a word of what he had been saying; and as she observed his dismay, she hastened to repair the wrong, turned a smiling face on him, and asked cheerily:

"You are very fond of music, aren't you?"

He stammered a faint "Yes," and from sheer vexation ate more than his fill of the chicken salad, and by the time the cake came was unable to swallow another bit. Ruth and the Baron, who were sitting up at the other end of the table, laughed and joked and seemed with every minute to advance in each other's favor.

It was a great relief to Varberg when the supper at length came to a close. He rose with such vehemence from the table that he came near upsetting his chair; then stepped on the dress of his little fair-haired damsel, begged her pardon, and hastily withdrew to a remote corner of the room. The music again scraped and twanged, and presently struck up a deliciously tuneful waltz, with that soft drowsiness in it which is so appropriate for an after-supper dance. Varberg stood mutely listening to its alluring murmur, and made sarcastic reflections upon every one who came within the reach of his eye. At last he came to the conclusion that he really disapproved of the whole company. There Weisskopf and Ruth whirled past him; and he noticed with a certain satisfaction that the Baron kicked out too much in the waltz, and that in fact his whole figure looked very ungraceful. However, Ruth smiled on him, and that was enough to make Varberg hate him. The music stopped rather abruptly, the dancers dispersed by couples through the adjoining rooms, and our Norseman looked at his watch and tried to steel his heart against all future vexations. Then, as he again raised his head, he saw Ruth hastening toward him all panting and aglow with heat and pleasure, and he keenly noted a certain vehemence in her motions and the superb singleness and purity in the combined lines of her neck and hair. He was secretly indignant at her for what he called "her flirtation with that German prize-fighter," but his wrath evaporated like the dew-drops in the sun, and he could only smile stupidly and distractedly pull at his watch-chain. With an almost sisterly frankness she addressed him, folded her hands confidingly over his arm, and looked up into his face with an air of mingled curiosity and tenderness. And all the time her silk gown kept up its vague rustle in his ear.

"Why do you stand here with that grand philosophical air, as if you felt above all these petty enjoyments which the rest of us are indulging in?"

"Ah, Miss Ruth, to tell the truth, everybody is stupid here to-night except you."

"Ah!" she exclaimed with a merry laugh. "Don't you believe that you can impose upon me in that way. No doubt you told Miss H——, whom you took to the table, the same story."

"It was just Miss H—— I was complaining of." And he gave her a grimly humorous description of his experience at the table. Ruth laughed again, but tried to excuse Miss H——.

"You can't expect everybody to be at home on the subject which happens to interest you. You ought to talk nonsense, and I can assure you, you will spend a charming evening. Now do just try it for once," she added coaxingly. "Just to please me. Come here; I will introduce you to a friend of mine in the Conversatory."

Before Varberg knew it, he found himself bowing before a yellow-haired little body with merry eyes, dressed in a low-necked blue silk gown, and with a large gold locket which rose and fell with the motion of her bosom. Ruth made some droll remark about the vast accomplishments of her friend, and said that she was convinced that she and Varberg would take kindly to each other. And away she went; decided in the twinkle of an eye a contest between two gentlemen each of whom insisted that she had promised the dance to him; and in the next moment Varberg saw her managing her trail in the lancers with the dignity of a queen.

The little yellow-haired lady proved more intelligent than Varberg had anticipated; her airy little remarks were like detached rose-leaves, so gently flushed and so delicate. He could not remember a word of their conversation the next morning: all he knew was that they had been mutually pleased with each other.

It was an hour after midnight, and the German was about to begin. Varberg bowed to his fair partner, and hastily betook himself to the next room, where he supposed Ruth would be waiting for him; when he had reached the door, however, he was met by Weisskopf, who took him aside into a corner, laid his arm half patronizingly about his neck, and whispered in his ear, "Miss Copley says she has promised the German to you, but I am persuaded that she would willingly dance it with me if you would release her."

Varberg colored to the edge to his hair, and involuntarily clenched his fists. "Is Miss Copley aware that you make me this proposition?" he asked with feigned coolness. Weisskopf shrugged his shoulders and assumed a mysterious air.

"Explain yourself," demanded Olaf aloud. "If Miss Copley knows anything about what you have said to me, you may tell her that she is bound by no obligation to me. If she is ignorant of it, then I can only say that I am astonished at your boldness, not to say impudence."

"We shall have a word with each other before

leaving this house," replied the Baron, shrugged his shoulders again, and went. Varberg well knew that this was about equal to a challenge; but as he had the near pleasure of a dance with Ruth before him, he forcibly banished the gloomy thought and troubled himself no more about it. He found his dark-haired queen sitting on a chair near the wall, her hands crossed in her lap and a pensive expression in her eyes; the moment she saw him her face brightened, and she arose and took his arm.

"I am glad you came," said she. "I don't like to be alone."

He was strangely oppressed at first, but no sooner had he wound his arm about her silken waist, and felt the tender luxury of her touch, her breath, and her voice as it were airily encircling him, than his senses were roused as from a trance; new and hitherto unknown sensations thrilled through his nerves like a tremulous rapture, and his heart beat to the ever-hastening measure of present and conscious bliss. Ruth chatted gaily and with a delightful *abandon* which was the more charming for the confidence it implied. She seemed not to have the remotest suspicion that she had herself been the cause of his displeasure. The fourth figure of the dance had just been finished and the fifth was about to begin. A gentleman, who held in his hand a wand with half a dozen variously colored streamers attached to it, bowed to Ruth, and a young lady held out a similar wand to Varberg. He chose an orange ribbon, and followed the train of gentlemen who had already made their choice. As they reached the middle of the floor, where the ladies were waiting, he noticed with pleasure that he had selected Ruth's color, but in the same moment some one quickly pulled the ribbon from his grasp, and presently he saw it in Weisskopf's hand. The ire rose within him; he stepped up to Ruth, whispered a word in her ear, and danced away with her.

"Blitz Donnerwetter," he heard some one exclaiming, and Ruth blushed slightly; but he heeded nothing.

Toward morning the party broke up, and as he was helping the ladies into the carriage, a German servant lifted his hat to him and delivered him a letter, the seal of which he instantly recognized. He quietly put it into his pocket, and ordered the coachman to drive.

"I may seem very inquisitive," said Ruth in an anxious voice, as he took his seat in the carriage; "but you will pardon me. What was that letter about?"

"I have not opened it yet," answered Varberg coolly.

Dearie was so exhausted that she could hardly keep her eyes open, and as soon as they came home she retired to her room. Ruth lit the lamp, and insisted upon his staying until he had got something to eat. And as they were seated together on the sofa, with a bottle of ale and a box of crackers before them, she anxiously repeated her question.

"Even at the risk of appearing rude," she said "I must beg of you to let me know what there is in that letter. I have my reasons for asking, and I shall never forgive you if you leave me in ignorance."

After some further coaxing, he pulled the fatal note from his pocket and gave it to her. Her hand trembled as she broke the seal, and in a low, excited voice she read as follows:

SIR: I demand satisfaction for the insults you have heaped upon me this evening. Unless within three days you ask my pardon in writing, you will meet me Friday afternoon at five o'clock, at Café Fr——, and you will there name me your second, and we shall further agree upon weapons, time, and place.

With true respect (*Mit wahrer Hochachtung*),
BARON MAX VON WEISSKOPF.

The letter dropped into her lap and she stared at him with a blank, frightened gaze. "You will ask his pardon, won't you?" she said at last beseechingly.

"Never," answered he fiercely.

"Not for my sake?" And she bent over toward him and seized his arm.

"Not for all the world."

"But it is merely a matter of form."

"Makes no difference."

She flung herself over into the corner of the sofa, covered her face with her hands, and burst into tears.

"Miss Ruth," cried he, while his emotion came near choking him. "I shall go mad if you don't stop crying. What is my life worth? There is not the thing in all the world which I wouldn't do for you." And as if frightened at his own words, he tore the door open and rushed out.

CHAPTER VII.

Ruth's Journal.

RUTH had promised her friends to keep a journal during her stay abroad, and then read it to them on her return. She began it much against her will, but after her acquaintance with Varberg her life seemed so much richer, and even the commonest events gained fresh import; and with every week her journal swelled in bulk. We make the following extracts:

June 3, 18—. Until yesterday I had really not been aware that I was in Europe. Now I begin to understand what Europe means; and strange to say, I owe it all to him—to my mysterious pursuer whom the beadle in St. Thomas's had to show out of the church. If any other man had done such a thing, I think I should have been angry with him; but the situation was really too comical, and his grand air and the imperturbable mien with which he marched down the aisle gained him my heartiest admiration. I knew I should meet him again, and still, I confess, I was frightened when I did meet him. His character is so perfectly in keeping with the spirit of mediæval times as I have imagined it, that it seems a pity that the modernized dress should refuse to carry out the illusion. And when I came so suddenly upon him in the forest under the Venusberg, I, certainly without knowing it, repaid him in his own coin; he pursued me three months ago into St. Thomas's; I unconsciously—or let me say deliberately, only to make the parallel perfect—followed his footsteps to this altar of nature, as I know he would have expressed it, and disturbed his devotion. May he and Lady Venus forgive me. But if I hadn't come, I have no doubt he would have shared the fate of Tannhaüser.

June 4, 18—. This morning I was waked up by the sound of music. I peeped through the curtain; I saw a whole orchestra of horn and stringed instruments stationed right under my window. They played Luther's hymn, " Ein' feste Burg ist unser Gott," and it was rendered with an artistic precision which I should have thought creditable in Thomas's orchestra. And these are but strolling street musicians! Ah *wie wunderschön!* It is Germany all over. Mr. Varberg did not call to-day, and I confess that I feel just a little bit disappointed.

June 7, 18—. He doesn't seem to be in a hurry about renewing the acquaintance. I shall treat him very stiffly when he does come. No, I won't either, for then I should betray that I have been thinking of him, and I wouldn't have him know that for anything.

June 9, 18—. He did call to-day, and we had a delightful walk through Rosenthal. I like him more, the more I see of him. There is a peculiar warmth and intensity in all that he says; his answers and even his most trifling remarks frequently startle me, and still they seem so natural that I wonder I didn't think of saying the very same thing myself.

June 11, 18—. We went to church together this morning. The minister laid down the law heavily, and described with a charming minuteness the tortures of the damned in hell. I feel confident that such a sermon could never have been preached in Boston—at least not in this century. Mr. Varberg was all devotion, and sat there as sober and as imperturbable as a rock. I was rather amused at the zeal of the old parson; and when he spoke about the seething tar, I couldn't help smiling; and still I was not really so irreverent as I seemed. As we left the church I asked Mr. Varberg if he believed in hell. He answered that he did, although hardly in the sense which this old preacher attached to it. I asked him in what sense then. Now I only wish I could repeat his answer just as he gave it, but I am afraid I can't. The meaning, however, was that God was all love, and would not condemn any man to eternal punishment. The man's life here developed a spiritual organism within him, which, if he had been wicked, would find its proper sphere beyond the grave in the society of the wicked, or what we call hell. Heaven would be wretchedness to him, and he would voluntarily seek the fellowship of those who shared his tastes and sympathies. Thus hell, although by no means happy, would afford, relatively speaking, the greatest happiness of which such men were capable. "Then," I answered thoughtlessly (and I am truly shocked at the irreverence of the remark), " I don't see why the devils in hell should not be quite as comfortable as the angels in heaven."

He looked at me half reproachfully, gave a brief polite answer, and changed the subject.

Now I should like to know why I always perforce must behave irreverently, not to say frivolously, in Mr. Varberg's presence. He evidently believes that there is not the thing in heaven or on earth which I have any respect for. And the fact that he believes this to be my character, in some mysterious way compels me to enter into the rôle which he kindly chooses to assign to me. I shouldn't wonder if it was sheer delicacy on my part, a fear of hurting his feelings by convincing him that he has been mistaken in his opinion of me.

June 13, 18—. We walked up through the fields along the river this afternoon, and there I saw for the first time in my life a stork. He stood pensively on one leg, just as in Hans Christian Andersen's stories. Mr. Varberg disapproved of the man who rode into town in a cart drawn by his wife and a big black dog. He sat coolly smoking on a sack of hay. I saw the color mounting to V.'s cheeks, and his behavior was so magnificent—I can find no other word for it—that I could not but feel grateful to him with all my heart. In his usual quiet manner he went to a tree, cut a huge whip, stripped off the leaves, and with the politest bow presented it to the man in the cart. The poor Teuton stared at him in stupid wonder, and his face was so pitiful to behold that I almost felt inclined to take his part. He tumbled out of his cart with a suddenness as if the whip had been applied to his own back, and walked off murmuring something between his teeth. Now who would have thought Mr. V. capable of such a joke? What especially amused me was the supreme coolness and dignity which he preserved during the whole performance. If I do or say anything ludicrous in his presence, I am always conscious of a vague sense of guilt; I know that he disapproves of me. Nevertheless it was very becoming to him.

June 16, 18—. O, if I only knew how I appear in his eyes; If I could only imagine what he thinks of me! I feel at times as if that calm blue eye of his was reading the most secret thoughts of my heart. I often think of what he said about authors. They have no business to have personal relations with their fellow mortals; they are not bound by the same obligations as other men. This was at least what I gathered from what he said to me that afternoon in Rosenthal. Now if it could be possible that it was merely this sort of literary interest he takes in me, I should at all events have to admit that he gave me fair warning. Oh, no, it can never be possible; it would be unworthy of him; he is incapable of doing anything so ungenerous. To steal into a young girl's heart only to decipher it, and coolly take his notes, while she suspected nothing! What am I saying? What has Mr. Varberg got to do with my heart? What does it matter to me whether he has a favorable or an unfavorable opinion of me? He is going away in three weeks, and I shall probably never see him again.

June 20, 18—. I have often said to myself that it is a matter of indifference to me what he thinks of me. I wish it was; but it isn't. I blame myself daily for appearing to him as it were in a false disguise. I am afraid of betraying what I think and feel, and therefore, against my will, I play the sceptic, and the consequence is that he believes me heartless and frivolous. And still there is a strange fascination about an assumed rôle. I think girls almost always have an instinct to conceal their real nature, and if for no other reason, then for the mere excitement of it. I know it is deceitful and wrong, but I can't help it.

June 23, 18—. I got angry with Mr. Varberg to-day, although I know it was very foolish of me. He said that what he especially liked about America was that there these delightful intellectual friendships could exist between men and women without leading necessarily to a more intimate relation. Here in Europe society frowned upon them, and no European woman was capable of appreciating such a mere intellectual devotion. I disliked the sentiment very much, and I came very near saying so; but I conquered myself and stammered a faint "Yes," and felt in my heart a detestable hypocrite. Why does he say such things to me? I wonder.

June 26, 18—. Turning over the leaves of my journal, I find that it is all full of Mr. Varberg. I didn't know that I had written so much about him. How can I read this to my friends it Boston when I return home? When they say to me, "Well, Ruth, read to us what you have seen in Europe," how mortifying to me, if I have to sit down and read to them about a young man by the name of Olaf Varberg. I like the name Olaf, although I don't know if I pronounce it right. It is so quaint.

June 27, 18—. I feel so strangely to day. I don't know what is the matter with me. Dearie tried to ridicule him, and said he looked as solemn as a deacon; then she insisted that he curled his hair and his moustache, and I am sure there isn't a word of truth in it. I told Dearie so too, but Dearie was in a contrary mood, and aggravated me beyond endurance, and somehow or other I couldn't manage her as well as usual. O dear! I wish he wouldn't come here any more. I can't bear to be teased about him; but I can't bear to have him stay away either.

CHAPTER VIII.

The Catastrophe.

IT was the day after the ball. Ruth was sitting at the window in the parlor, pensively resting her chin upon her folded hands. Her cheeks were very pale, and her long, dark lashes hid the anxious glance of the eyes.

"It was very foolish in me to cry last night," she thought, "and if he comes to-day, I shall do my best to bewilder him. What could he think of me?"

Nevertheless her heart was heavy, although she was loath to admit it, even to herself; she was rather provoked at herself for taking such a lively interest in his doings. All the night the thought of Varberg had haunted her; she had seen him lying half dead on the green grass, the light quenched in his eye, the paleness of death upon his cheeks and his parted lips, and the gore darkening his blonde locks. And she imagined herself bending down over him, folding his hands upon his breast, and kissing his cold forehead, while her tears fell hot and fast upon his face. Now, if Varberg had actually been dead, she might have done all this; at all events, she would sincerely have mourned him; but unhappily he was yet alive, and she was angry with him. It seemed especially hard to forgive him that he had been witness to that involuntary outburst of emotion on her part—nay, that he had, although through no fault of his own, been the occasion of it.

"If he chooses to kill himself, or have somebody else kill him, what does that matter to me?" she asked herself repeatedly, and she came to the cheerful conclusion that Varberg's life or death concerned her no more than the man in the moon.

Then there was a knock at the door, and a quick flush shot over Ruth's cheeks. Varberg entered; she advanced to the middle of the floor and shook hands with him. He seemed more than usually grave and reserved; and she noticed the newness of all he had on, even to the silk hat and the gloves; he impressed her as a man who was going to his own funeral. Various indifferent topics of conversation were taken up and again dropped. The words froze as they fell from the lips, and each seemed to be pursuing his own track of thought unaided and unaccompanied by the other.

"You are so strange to-day, Mr. Varberg," said Ruth at last.

"I confess I feel a little oppressed; I came here to you to be cheered."

"How shall I cheer you then? What do you propose to do?"

"Anything you like."

"Well, then let us abuse our friends," said she with a kind of joyous vehemence. "I know of nothing that is more apt to cheer me."

"I don't know that we have any friends in common," replied Varberg with a faint smile. "And for each to abuse his own, when his good points would hardly be appreciated by the other, would be very unprofitable work."

"Certainly we have friends in common; there is, for instance, Weisskopf, the Baron."

"Well, what do you think of him?" And the gloom again gathered on Varberg's brow.

"Perhaps you don't know that he called

here this morning and asked for you. He had been at your rooms, but did not find you. I invited him in, and like all Germans he smokes detestable tobacco. I have been airing the room for several hours since he left. Indeed, he sat puffing away like a young steam-engine."

"But that hardly expresses your opinion of him. If you wish to cultivate his acquaintance, you have to accept him as a Teuton, or not at all."

"Mr. Varberg," cried Ruth laughing, "I haven't accepted him in any sense whatever. He is to me simply a phenomenon; and as such I enjoy him, and dismiss him when I find him no more entertaining."

"Is that the way you do with all your friends?"

"Certainly. But some of my friends I hope will continue to entertain me as long as I live. You can't blame me for speaking in this way. You have taught it me yourself. To you, if I may trust your own words, men are merely psychological phenomena, and I with the rest. Now I am beginning to profit by your teachings."

Varberg made no answer; but his eye rested half reproachfully on Ruth, and he silently cursed the fate that had made her so fair. There was a feverish uneasiness in her gayety that pained and distressed him. "What can have wrought this change in her?" he questioned himself; and then added with a sigh, "*Femina semper mutabile et varium.*" It was a comforting thought that it was merely the experience of the whole world which was repeating itself in him. Ruth in the meanwhile, piqued at his silence, went on in the same strain.

"Weisskopf," she said, "is an exceedingly entertaining phenomenon. But there is something of the adventurer about him, which, however, makes him no less interesting as a phenomenon. I regret to say that I always distrust him; and especially when he talks about his own gallant deeds, I am aware that he does not always expect to be pinned down to a literal interpretation. Then he has a way of paying one the most ridiculous compliments with a *hauteur* and a magnificence which border on the sublime. My own opinions, if I have the impudence to have any, he treats with a gentle forbearance which would irritate me beyond endurance, if I didn't find the situation novel enough to be interesting. My serious remarks he listens to with an indulgent smile, and then leaves them unanswered or dismisses them with a jest, as if they were too insignificant to merit his attention. And the end of it invariably is that I am somehow or other compelled to assume the rôle which he pleases to give me, and I feel like an irresponsible child, and even talk and act like one. But Mr. Varberg, you are not listening to me," she cried, after a moment's pause. "Whither are your thoughts wandering? Is it the fair-haired maidens of Norway you are dreaming about?"

"You do me injustice, Miss Copley," answered he, rising from the sofa. "But I have no doubt the fresh air would do us both good, after the exertions of yesterday. Would you not favor me with your company?"

"Certainly," she answered, and walked toward the door. "In the meanwhile, while I put on my hat, you may amuse yourself with the 'Leipziger Tageblatt.' Here it is. There is a picture in it of a Russian Internationalist, who has run away from St. Petersburg with a large amount of money, and the description as well as the picture, as my aunt remarked this morning, bears a strong resemblance to you. So you had better be on your guard, or you might be sent to Siberia."

And she laughed a loud, unnatural laugh, and ran out of the room. He took up the paper, and found there a portrait which really did not look unlike him. What especially startled him was the notice that the criminal had a slight scar over his right eye, which was another point of resemblance. Ruth returned. He laid the paper away, and thought no more of it. On the staircase they met Mrs. Elder and Dearie, who had been out shopping; they stopped for a moment, exchanged the usual greetings, and parted.

It was late in the afternoon, and the broad gravel paths of Rosenthal were almost empty. Here and there a couple of students lay idly smoking on the grass, and in some thick-leafed copse a loose-coated journeyman lingered in amorous luxury with the mistress of his heart. The air was rich and warm, and a luminous, misty gauze spread a faint glamour through the atmosphere. Swarms of gnats hovered in an airy dance under the sunny linden crowns, and the murmurous music of their wings imperceptibly blended with the summer stillness; and now and then a large black insect buzzed with "heedless hum" across the path, and lost itself in the gloom of a neighboring thicket. It was difficult to think of the new world, with its busy life and its noisy bustle, on a day like this; indeed, it seemed hard to persuade one's self that Wall Street and Broadway were not all a dream, a grotesque invention of a capricious fancy. These were at least Varberg's reflections, and even Ruth's mind was gently attuned; she forgot the resentment she had lately harbored against her friend, and began to talk in her old easy, confidential way.

"Now, Mr. Varberg," said she, "you know me too well to be angry with me, if I return once more to this fatal subject. But tell me truly and honestly whether you think that a man's honor can be saved by his having his ear or his nose cut off, or his face disfigured by an unsightly scar?"

"An honest question deserves an honest answer," replied he. "In the abstract, I disapprove of duelling as decidedly as you do. But a time-honored custom, which has been handed down to us by our forefathers, we cannot afford to ignore."

"Aha," ejaculated she; "then it is your romantic notions of chivalry that interfere with your better judgment! And truly, if it were for the honor of some beloved maiden that you drew your sword, I should myself find some excuse for it. But, after all, losing your life for your lady love, or rescuing her from death and then marrying her, is a very old-fashioned sort of thing, and as a theme of fiction it has been so well worn out by our novelists and romancers that at last nobody really believes in it. If I should want to sacrifice my life, I should invent some other way which nobody had ever tried before."

"And how do you know that it is not for the sake of some beloved maiden that I propose to fight?"

She turned her head abruptly, and a deep blush mounted to her cheeks.

"If you were a German," she began, with her face still averted, "I should not attempt to contradict you. But you are an American citizen, and are not bound to conform to the customs of the Germans."

"True; but when you are in Rome you do as the Romans do."

The evening wore on, and without heeding whither their steps carried them, they hastened forward. The last red glow of the sunset lay like a band of flame along the horizon, and the moon, as if by surprise, burst forth full and clear from behind its vapory citadel; it spread its lustre over the dim blue sky, and the thin clouds were fringed with a pale, ghostly gold. Now and then some lonely quail raised its shrill cry from the distant meadows, the crickets chirped drowsily in the grass, and a warm summer wind breathed with a faint rushing through the crowns of the beeches and linden trees.

"I wonder where we are?" said Ruth, laying her hand upon his arm. "It seems all so strange and unfamiliar."

"I don't think I have ever been here before," answered Varberg, while he gently drew her arm through his. "But nevertheless this whole landscape appears to me so remotely familiar, that I cannot but think that I must have seen it somewhere, perhaps in a dream or in a vision. And if I had seen you here for the first time, I should have recognized you at once, for you are as much a part of the landscape as the linden trees and the chirp of the crickets."

"Ah, you flatter me," she replied musingly, "although," she added with a smile, "the comparison with the crickets ought not to make me vain. But if you will listen to my chirp, I think it is high time that we think of finding our way home."

Ruth and Varberg had both a talent for losing their way. When in each other's company they forgot everything except their own happiness. Now they wandered about through the broad moonlit avenues, in the vague hope of sometime reaching the city. The vast calm of the night, the placid massiveness of the shadows and the fragile woof of cloud, which spread like a fairy frostwork over the sky, chimed together into a world-wide, silent chant, a voiceless melody of wonder. And although he felt the stillness sinking into his heart and diffusing its blessed sense of peace through his whole being, he was still conscious of one wakeful, dimly-defined desire, which came and went, and ever evaded the grasp of his thought. It was as if he expected a miracle to be wrought somehow, without his own agency; and whenever he looked up into Ruth's eyes, and saw her fair young face smitten into marble by the rays of the moon, he believed that the miracle was near, and the blood throbbed more swiftly through his pulses. At length they saw the roofs of the city shimmering between the leaves, and the fatal confession hovered upon his lips; but just at that moment they heard harsh laughter close by, and caught sight of two men, one of whom stood leaning against the trunk of a tree, while the other lay outstretched upon the grass. The more able-bodied of the two helped his companion to his feet, and they both reeled out into the road.

"Come, let us go back and take another way," said Ruth, drawing her veil down over her face.

"You are not afraid of two miserable drunkards, I hope?" answered Varberg, and walked on.

The men steered straight against them.

"Ah, mein Liebchen," said the one, and

Varberg in an instant recognized Weisskopf's voice, although it was unnaturally hoarse and drowsy. "Don't make yourself so precious;" and he stretched out his arm to pull away the veil from Ruth's face.

"Step aside," cried Varberg, "or I'll strike you down on the spot."

"Strike me down on the spot—ah?" droned the Baron in the same drunken tone. "You are in a fighting mood, are you?"

Ruth stood pale and erect, but she trembled over her whole body. Weisskopf made another stretch toward her, but before he had time to reach her Varberg sprang forward, seized him by the throat, threw him down on the ground, and put his knees on his chest.

"Now, you impudent wretch," said he in a hoarse whisper, "if you dare stir, I shall strike you dead."

The Baron's companion in the meanwhile stood howling "Police," at the top of his voice, and while the victim still lay groaning in the powerful grip of his assailant's fist, Varberg felt himself suddenly seized by the shoulders and violently flung over to the other side of the road.

He had hardly time to recover from his surprise, when he was again grabbed by the neck, and found himself struggling in the arms of two burly Teutons in policemen's uniforms. Weisskopf, who had been considerably sobered by the sudden encounter, rose to his feet, and explained to the policemen that he had been unexpectedly assaulted, and he was just recounting the details of the affair when Ruth stepped close up to him, lifted her veil, and gazed him in the eye. He tumbled backward, as if hit by an invisible hand, and staggered away between the trees; his companion followed. Varberg vainly attempted to conciliate the officers of the law; and Ruth, her voice choked with emotion, prayed them to let him depart in peace. But the Teutons, in their official zeal, were deaf to all remonstrances, and hustled their victim about as if he had been the most atrocious criminal in the world.

"Yes, yes, we know all about it," roared one of them. "We have long been on the track of you; and we knew we should find you at last. You will have a chance of explaining all that to-morrow."

"But I protest. I am an American citizen."

"You can protest to-morrow."

"Then allow me at least," said Varberg calmly, " to procure a carriage for this lady. She has, at all events, nothing to do with this. Moreover, you need not tear me to pieces. I shall follow you of my own accord."

After a brief consultation they decided to grant this request, and without more ado they conducted Ruth down to the corner of Frankfurter Strasse, where a carriage was found.

"My dear Miss Ruth," said Varberg, as they were about to part, "don't let this disturb you. To-morrow it will all be cleared up, and I shall come at once to see you."

"Ah, Mr. Varberg," answered she, while a tear glittered in her eye, "all these indignities you have to suffer on my account. O dear, what shall I do?"

The policemen slammed the door to, and hurried him off. An hour later he sat on a hard wooden bench, in a narrow prison cell, and philosophized on the vanity of human happiness. A damp, musty smell of masonry pervaded the air, and in spite of the warmth he shivered.

The moonlight streamed in through the small iron-barred window, high up on the wall, and a narrow strip of pale blue sky, dimmed by the dingy glass, gazed in upon him, and mocked him with its vague suggestion of freedom. A month earlier, when visiting Wartburg, he had imagined himself in the romantic capacity of a prisoner; now the dreary reality stared him in face, and the romance had utterly vanished. The jailer brought him a quarter section of a black bread and a jug of water, but he refused to touch either. He heard the rattling of chains somewhere at the other end of the corridor; the door of his cell was locked and barred on the outside, and the retiring steps of the jailer re-echoed with an uncomfortable regularity and sharpness under the stone vaults.

It was after midnight when at last he threw himself down on his straw mattress, and toward morning he fell asleep. He dreamed that he was at Wartburg, and that he was sitting under a huge poplar at the foot of the Venusberg. The leaves of the poplar clanked with strange metallic voices, which fell upon his ear like the subdued tinkling of a vast chorus of infinitely small bells. Hard by stood a couple of fragrant, maidenly birches, which breathed forth an anxious hush, and rustled faintly and soothingly. but under the birch copse grew clusters of ghostly flowers, which, eagerly raised their fragile cups of crimson, ruby, and amethyst toward the silent moon, and gathered its rays, until they were filled to the brim; and then they bent their heads droopingly to the earth, and vanished like a spark that is quenched. All of a sudden, while Varberg sat gazing upon this wondrous spectacle, the hill was rent in twain, and there sat Lady Venus on her golden throne, and beckoned to him with a joyous smile on her countenance. A delicious shudder ran through his frame; he arose, and stood for a moment wavering. Lady Venus arose, too, and descended from her throne, and now he saw that it was Ruth. He rushed forward to throw himself at her feet, but out of the ground there came an old man with a gray moustache, and that was the faithful Eckart, but it was also Olaf's own grandfather, whom he had left behind him in Norway.

"Flee, youth, flee," cried the old man; "in her embrace lurk death and eternal damnation."

Varberg turned to fly; but first he would look once more upon that young joyous face; and the longer he looked the fairer she grew, and the harder it became to part from her.

"Death and damnation," cried the faithful Eckart, and Olaf summoned all his strength and tore himself away; but a net of fine invisible threads seemed to wind itself about his arms and feet, until at length he could not advance an inch further. Turning once more, he saw that her hair had grown to an immense length, and encompassed the woods far and near.

"Flee now, if thou canst," said she with the same joyous smile, and the voice was Ruth's. He rushed back, thrust down his old grandfather, and in an ineffable rapture clasped her tightly to his breast. The hill closed behind him, and in the same moment he awoke. There were the bare stone walls, the iron-barred window, and a belated star which still glimmered feebly on the sky. He was indeed a prisoner, but in the Leipsic jail, not in the Venusberg.

CHAPTER IX.

To the Rescue.

AT ten o'clock the next morning Varberg was summoned to appear before the police court. The judge, a moon-faced, bald-headed man of a very imposing front, sat behind the bar, and the Baron von Weisskopf, the traces of yesterday's carousal still visible on his countenance, was on the witness stand. The usual questions about name, position, etc., were promptly answered. "You say that this gentleman attacked you in Rosenthal," said the judge to Weisskopf.

"I do, your honor," replied the latter, while he reddened to the edge of his hair, and was evidently very much ashamed of himself.

"With an intent to rob you?"

"I think not, your honor; I should rather say that he was slightly drunk, and didn't know exactly what he was doing."

Varberg sent the Baron a keen, scornful look; but he disdained to contradict him, for fear of implicating Ruth in an affair that would necessarily bring her into an unpleasant position, and which after all could lead to nothing worse than a fine of five or ten dollars. After some further cross-examination, the case was dismissed, and Varberg paid his fine on the spot. He was just about to leave the court when one of the policemen who had assisted at his arrest rushed up to the judge, laid a photograph down on the desk before him, and began to talk and gesticulate eagerly. Varberg finally concluded that he must be the subject of their discussion, for the judge now glanced at him, and now again at the photograph; as he was about to depart, the policeman called him back, and ordered him to remain.

"You say that you are an American citizen," said his honor. "Have you any passport to show that this is actually the case?"

"Passports are no longer used in civilized countries," replied Olaf. "I have none."

The judge raised his eyebrows, and nodded significantly to the policeman.

" You don't happen to know the name Fedor Voriakoff?" continued he.

" I do not, sir."

" And you have never been in Russia ? "

" Never."

Quick as lightning flashed through the unfortunate Norseman's brain what Ruth had told him the day before about his resemblance to the Russian Internationalist. He suddenly grew very red in his face ; the judge noticed it, nodded again contentedly, and said :

"At all events, we shall have to detain you here, until you can prove to us satisfactorily who you are."

" That may be very difficult, sir, as I have no friends here in Leipsic."

The policeman in the meanwhile took the measure of Varberg's height, and narrowly viewed his face, all of which our hero endured with a calm composure, well worthy of the Viking race. After some more questioning and other ceremonies he was conducted back to the cell which he had previously occupied. He demanded pen and ink, and immediately sat down to write a note to the American consul, stating his difficulty, and asking what he had to do. Toward evening he received a polite reply, informing him that, as he had no papers to prove his citizenship, he, the consul, had no means of helping him.

Two days later everything was disorder and confusion in the house with the old-fashioned archway. The vacation had commenced, and Mrs. Elder and her nieces had received an invitation to come and spend the summer with some friends in England. Half-packed trunks and a half a dozen bandboxes of various sizes and colors lay scattered about on the floor, and the tables and chairs were covered with books, hats, ribbons, and freshly ironed skirts and dresses. Dearie was running about the room busying herself with packing, and Ruth was sitting at the window in her usual attitude, resting her chin upon her folded hands. Her face wore a grave, almost sad expression; her cheeks were pale, and her eyes looked large and lustrous. Suddenly she arose, then stopped in the middle of the floor, as if struggling with some great resolution. She hastily put on her hat, threw a light shawl about her shoulders, and walked toward the door.

"Ruth, where are you going?" cried Dearie. "Supper will be ready in a few minutes."

"I am going out to take a walk."

"This is indeed a most extraordinary time for taking a walk," replied the cousin. "If I were you, I should certainly not trouble myself so much about a man whom I had hardly known for four weeks."

"Fortunately you don't know what I am troubling myself about," said Ruth scornfully, and hastened away. Dearie was mystified; she could not imagine how this change had come over her cousin; why she was so pale and distracted, and why she had walked about as in a dream the whole day. But Dearie contented herself with exclaiming, "Well, I must say!" and went on packing. If she had read the Leipsic paper for that morning, she might perhaps have found the clue to the mystery.

Ruth hurried up one street and down another; her feet were as if benumbed; the ground seemed to swell and again to sink beneath her tread, and she hardly knew where she was stepping. Unconsciously she pressed her lips together, and kept her eyes steadfastly fixed on the stones in the pavement. She could not get rid of the feeling that she was doing something wrong, or at least unwomanly, and now and then she cast a shy glance at some passer-by, as if fearing that her face should betray her secret. With a beating heart she mounted the broad stone staircase of the jail, and inquired of the woman who was sweeping the hall, where she could find the jailer. The woman looked wonderingly at her, then murmured something between her teeth, and after some minutes returned with a rough, ruddy-bearded Hercules who held a large bunch of keys in his hand.

"What do you want?" asked he brusquely, striking the keys against his thigh.

"I want to see a friend," answered Ruth in a low voice.

"Have you a permit?"

"No; I didn't know that it was necessary."

"I can't let you in without that. You may perhaps get one from the assistant master of the police in the office across the street."

And he turned his back on her, and marched away, rattling violently with his keys.

Ruth crossed the street and entered the office. There were two or three showily dressed gentlemen standing at the bar talking with the officer. She pulled her veil down over her face; and seated herself at the door in the hope that they would soon go away. But they took their time; and at last the officer locked his desk, and put on his hat. She had to conquer her pride; advanced to the bar, and in a voice which, in spite of her efforts, trembled a little, she asked for permission to visit the supposed Russian prisoner.

"What is your relation to him?" asked the master of the police. "Are you his wife?"

"No," she stammered feebly; her face burned as with fever, and she felt as if she were going to sink into the floor.

"What are you then?" inquired her tormentor harshly.

"I am his friend."

"Ah, she is his friend," repeated he, turning to the gentlemen, who both glanced insolently at her, and then burst into laughter. "No, we don't admit *friends.*"

That was too much for her. Her indignation was kindled within her, and her womanly wrath mastered her grief. She threw her veil back, raised her head, and advanced a step toward the officer.

"Sir," said she, in a tone which at once demanded respect, "what right have you to insult a lady who comes here to ask of you what it is not in your power to deny her? The gentleman whom I wish to see has been convicted of no crime, and his case is simply that of mistaken identity. Now he needs the assistance of his friends to prove who he is. If you refuse me admission, I shall procure it to-morrow through the American consul; and I shall take care to have your behavior toward me duly reported."

The Teuton was not a little bewildered at this unexpected outburst. He stood for a minute with a perplexed frown on his brow, as if meditating whether he ought to be angry or not; then, with a surly mien, he scratched his name to a printed permit, and handed it to Ruth. The sun was near its setting as she reached the street;

she again entered the gloomy edifice, and hastened onward through the dark, cool vaults. She presented her paper at the jailer's lodge, and was conducted by the same ruddy-bearded Hercules through a labyrinth of corridors, stairs, and galleries, until at length they stopped at a small door, which was heavily bolted, and moreover secured by a huge iron bar.

"Ah," thought Ruth, "here he has had to spend three long days, and all on my account, because he was good, and brave, and generous!"

The door groaned on its hinges as the jailer pushed it open. Ruth steeled her nerves, and determined not to give away to any grief or emotion. She peered into the cell, and by the glimmer of the departing daylight saw a stooping figure seated on a wooden stool, close to the wall. He did not stir as she entered, but remained in the same attitude, with his head resting on his hands. A sudden fright seized her; she bent down over him, laid her hand on his shoulder, and whispered, "Mr. Varberg!" He sprang up—then again staggered backward against the wall.

"Miss Ruth!" he exclaimed. "Can I trust my eyes?"

"Yes, Mr. Varberg," answered she, "it is I. I have come here to see what I can do to get you away from this horrible place. We are all going to start for France and England in a few days; so, you see there is no time to be lost."

"It is very kind of you to think of me in my present misfortune; but I am afraid nothing can be done. I have given up all hope. I shall probably have to go to Russia, and there they will find out their mistake; but I thank you a thousand times for coming to tell me good-by."

"I did not come to tell you good-by, and still less did I come to be thanked," answered Ruth calmly (and he did not suspect what that calmness cost her); "I came to consult with you, and then to act. First, have you no official document, issued in the United States, or any communication from people who are known to the authorities here?"

He opened his eyes widely—it was strange to hear her talk in that calm, practical way—and after some hesitation he replied:

"No; nothing that I can think of."

"Have you not a letter of credit?"

"Certainly."

"And where is it?"

"It is in my desk, at my lodgings."

"Then, please write a note to your landlady requesting her to send me this letter of credit at once. Or better, if you will give me the key to the desk, I will send for it myself. You have probably drawn money on it several times since your arrival here?"

"Every other week, for the last six months."

"Then leave the rest to me. By to-morrow night you shall be out. Now, good-night. I can never hope to repay the debt I owe you!" and she reached out her hand to him. He seized it and pressed it to his lips; but the hand was cold, and it trembled. Varberg was deeply moved. How cruelly had he not judged and misunderstood this young girl! There she stood, apparently proud and erect, and talked in a composed, business-like way, while the cold perspiration burst from her brow, and her frame trembled with suppressed emotion. If it had not been ungenerous to take advantage of this moment's excitement, he would have thrown himself at her feet, and begged her to forgive and to love him. He still held her hand in both his, and looked up into her large dark eyes, which glistened with the lustre of a gathering tear. He noticed a slight nervous quivering of the upper lip, but otherwise her features showed no sign of unusual feeling.

"Ah, Miss Ruth," said he warmly, "how good and how noble you are, and how sadly I have misjudged you!"

"I am not so good as you think," answered she, attempting to smile. "Good night!"

The rusty hinges groaned; with a sharp click the key turned in the lock, and with a heavy thump the iron bar was pushed before the door. He strained his ear to catch the sound of her receding footsteps; but they were too light—he did not hear them. He sprang forward and struck his hand against his forehead.

"Good God!" cried he, staring around him on the gray, naked walls. "Where am I?"

He threw himself down on the hard straw mattress, covered his face with his hands, and breathed heavily. He had hardly tasted of food for two days, and overwhelmed with weariness and exhaustion, he fell into a troubled, feverish sleep.

It is hardly necessary to recount in detail Ruth's adventures during the next day, and the means by which she procured her friend's release. Having obtained the letter of credit, she called on the banker with whom Varberg had his account, briefly stated to him what had happened, and asked for his assistance. She called his attention to the fact that the letter was dated December last, while the Russian criminal, according to the advertisement, had not disappeared until March of the present year, which in itself was sufficient proof that the two persons could not be identical. The banker, moved by her beauty and her earnestness, rather than by any sympathy for the persecuted Norseman, promised her to present the case at once to the authorities. But justice is slow in Germany, as elsewhere, and it was not until nearly ten o'clock in the evening that the herculean jailer, accompanied by an assistant of the police, opened the door of Varberg's cell, and told him that he was at liberty to depart. He was not American enough at that moment to think of claiming redress or satisfaction; his only thought was whether Ruth had left Leipsic or not, and the only redress he wished was an hour's happiness with her.

It was a dark night, and a thick, impenetrable fog brooded over the empty streets. The watchman's horn sounded from the cupola of the court-house and startled a feeble echo from the opposite side of the square, and the watchman of St. Thomas's answered with a long, dolorous note. The lantern in the church steeple hung as if suspended in mid-air, and glimmered faintly in the dreary solitude of the fog. Varberg rushed like a madman through the desolate city. His head swam; he felt faint and dizzy, and his knees almost refused to support the burden of his body. Nevertheless all his soul was filled with one strong desire, and this desire imparted strength to his tottering limbs. He hastily crossed the promenade, swung himself over the garden fence, and stood anxiously peering through the gloom. The great dusky façade of the building stared upon him with a spectre-like frown, and the last spark of hope was quenched within him. No friendly light beckoned to him from her window. She slept—all the city slept—all was gloom and desolation.

Hour after hour he wandered about in the wet garden, now slipping in the muddy walks, now stumbling over a flower-bed or a tree root. The lilacs shook their cold tears over his head; the night folded him in its clammy arms, and pressed its chilly kiss upon his forehead, until he shuddered through every nerve and fibre. An intolerable hunger tormented him, and his hands and feet were benumbed with cold and exhaustion; but all hotels and restaurants were closed, and moreover he had forgotten to reclaim his purse and his papers, of which he had been deprived at the time of his arrest. Toward morning he sauntered wearily to his lodgings, and by the watchman's assistance gained access to the house. His landlady, dressed in a light light negligée, met him in the hall, and was so frightened at his appearance that she came near fainting.

"*Mein lieber Doctor, wo sind sie doch gewesen!*" cried she, as she recovered her senses.

"*Ich bin im Gefängniss gewesen,*" answered he absently.

During the greater part of that day he slept, and when, toward evening, he sought the house with the archway, the nest was empty and the bird had flown.

CHAPTER X.

The Clock Strikes.

DURING the next week time hung heavily on Varberg's hands; hour after hour he went aimlessly strolling through Rosenthal, and when he became weary of this kind of amusement he would drop into some random restaurant, where he was sure of finding acquaintances, and there he would sit distractedly devouring one dish of ice-cream after the other, and passively suffer himself to be imposed upon by waiters and fellow students. His unexpected arrest had prevented him from meeting the Baron at the time appointed, and his further apprehensions regarding the duel were at last removed by a note from his opponent, dated Fulda, in which the writer informed him that "circumstances" had compelled him to leave the city, and that consequently he withdrew his challenge. Here he was even deprived of the opportunity to perform an heroic act, which in some measure would have relieved the dreary emptiness of his existence; for if he had fought the duel, it would have been done for Ruth's sake, and if he had been offered the chance of refusing it, it would have been an equally heroic deed, which she would have treasured up in her heart, and which would have raised him in her estimation. But fate persisted in turning his tragic plots into farces, and he had no choice but to accept the humiliating position of a farcical hero. In another week the University *semester* would close, and he would point his course northward, where his old grandparents and his sister were eagerly awaiting him. Strange to say, however, within these last weeks all his enthusiasm for his native land, with its rugged rocks and its fair-haired damsels, had cooled, and he became seriously alarmed at the prospect of appearing among his relatives in this new character of an apathetic cosmopolitan.

Leipsic seemed the mere wraith of its own self after Ruth had gone. The mornings were what a romanticist would have termed "impudently awake," the noonday hour was as if lulled into a heavy fever doze, and the sultry night gave neither rest nor comfort. It lasted some time before he reached the conclusion that Ruth must have left so suddenly because she didn't desire to see him; he would have gladly dismissed the thought of such a duplicity, as he called it, on her part, but a hundred unwelcome arguments thronged to its support, until he was forced to accept the situation, humiliating though it be. He had noticed that she treated him coldly the day after that fatal ball, and the reason for this he sought in the little scene in the night when she had in his presence yielded to a burst of grief, of emotion, or of nervousness, or God knows what it was; and he had ungenerously accepted it as an evidence of her interest in him, and had then fled like a coward, perhaps, because he feared that a delay would necessarily have led him to betray those feelings which, as he flattered himself, he had hitherto scrupulously concealed. She had humiliated herself before him: what then could be more natural than that she wished to get as far away from him as possible? That she had exerted herself in his behalf, and procured his release from the arrest, might have been a deliberate and even a selfish act. She had herself been the innocent cause of his imprisonment, and a simple sense of justice and duty had impelled her to explain the misunderstanding. She would not yield him the privilege of suffering for her sake; he was to have no claim upon her sympathies, perhaps not even upon her friendship and her gratitude. It was this gloomy train of thought which incessantly occupied Varberg's fancy during the last week of his stay at Leipsic. "Alas," said he to himself, as he promenaded meditatively up and down on the floor, "our account is even, our tale is told." And that same night he wrote a poem which began thus:

    A sleepless, joyless—nay, and deathless passion!

A few days before his departure he received letters from Norway, in which his grandfather, grandmother, and Brynhild (each according to his or her own fashion) expressed their joy at the prospect of seeing him. It made him feel wretched and guilty, for he could not but consider how little he had done to merit the endearing names they bestowed upon him. How little had he thought of them during these many months while they had been counting the days until his return! And even now, although he acknowledged the injustice, he was as powerless as ever to repair it. In a state of utter disgust, he at length boarded the train which was to take him by way of Frankfort to Strasbourg, whence he expected to continue the journey to Paris, then cross the channel, and take steamer from London to Norway. As the train moved out of the depot, a party of students began to sing: " Wo ist des Deutschen Vaterland ? " and Varberg involuntarily applied the sentiment of the song to himself, and profoundly sympathized with this poet, who, without intending it, has expressed so strikingly how vague to a German mind is the idea of the German fatherland.

The wheels rattled away over the rails, the smoke whirled past the windows, and the jolly companions in the next car kept up an incessant brawl, and seemed nothing daunted either by the heat or by the ingenious discomfort of their quarters. Varberg being alone with an old gentleman in his *coupé*, pressed himself up into a corner, shut his eyes, and allowed his mind to roam idly wherever it listed. First he imagined himself writing a letter to Ruth, in which he assumed an air of cheerful unconcern, assured her in the politest phrases of his heartfelt interest in all her doings, and expressed the hope that the future might afford him an opportunity of proving how highly he prized her good opinion and her friendship. Such a letter would evidently remove all fear of further misunderstandings, and would no doubt rehabilitate him in her estimation. And however much his literary half, which was fond of asserting its independence, approved of this plan, his more human self condemned it as a piece of dishonesty and cowardice. Moreover, there was this obstacle, that he had no idea of where Ruth was, and had consequently no means of reaching her. It was the helplessness of his situation, or, more probably, the gloominess of the prospect which lay before him—a long, empty life without her—which called up to his mind the thought of death. In an altogether irresponsible mood he let one fancy succeed another, until he imagined himself dead, and saw Ruth sitting in the parlor in Leipsic, with the morning paper in her hand;

suddenly she turns pale, starts up with a frightened look, and hastens out of the room. In an hour she returns: but her eyes are red and swollen, and her upper lip quivers just a little, as it always did whenever she tried to conquer an overwhelming emotion. Mrs. Elder anxiously inquires what has happened, and Ruth points silently to the paper, which Mrs. Elder gazes at with a profound air, although she cannot read a word of it. Varberg found this a very pleasing kind of a reverie, and took a fierce satisfaction in thinking that now, when it was too late, she had at last discovered his worth. After all, what greater happiness could he desire than to have her shed tears over him, and to have her cherish a tender, regretful memory of him? These were the reflections of Varberg the author, who was at times not free from sentimentality. "And then she would go and marry somebody else," suggested a prosaic voice in his breast, and he had to own that this was only too probable, which at once cut short the reverie.

In the evening he took supper in Frankfort, and reached Strasbourg about four o'clock the following morning. He took up his lodgings in the Inn of the Holy Spirit, on account of its association with Goethe's youth, although it was by no means the best hotel in the city. He left orders to be waked up at eight, but the servant was probably too sleepy to understand him; and to his utter disgust, he found that it was not far from noon when finally he was roused by the jingling of a bell out in the hall. He made a hasty toilet, and a still hastier breakfast, consulted his guide-book in regard to the situation of the Cathedral, and started out in the hope that his good instinct would lead him by the directest way to the object of his search. He bestowed but a passing glance upon the time-blackened fronts of the houses, with their queer old-worldish look and their many-gabled waywardness; the pretty Alsatian girls, in their picturesque attire, with the white embroidered aprons, half covering the front of their short skirts, interested him but little. He noticed that most of them carried hymn-books and a folded handkerchief in their hands, which reminded him of the possibility of its being Sunday. And immediately a Sabbath feeling stole over him; he noticed a certain festive look in the gray houses, and in the freshly swept streets; the sky looked serener, the sunshine clearer, and nature seemed to be breathing with a fuller breast than before. He unconsciously slackened his speed and bent his head, and half forgot where he was going, when suddenly a mighty rush of metallic clangor fell upon the silence like an avalanche, startling the repose of a mountain ravine into a cataract of sonorous thunder. Varberg swiftly raised his eyes—and for an instant he lost his breath. There, is the broad, affluent light of the noonday, rose the solemn presence of the minster with its sculptured façade, serenely grave, majestic, and withal joyous and fantastically graceful. He had indeed, as Lowell says, "taken his minster unawares."

The lofty spire climbed, with grand aspiration, far and ever farther up into the pure blue space, and as his spirit caught its ethereal suggestion, a proud sense of kinship stirred in the Norseman's bosom, and an exhilarating thrill of happiness shot through his nerves. His frame seemed to swell into larger proportions; he involuntarily raised his head, and his breast expanded with a magnificent consciousness of strength. The artistic purpose of his life assumed a fresh magnitude, and mere personal concerns appeared small and sordid, and faded away into nothingness.

"Thank heaven, I have at last found my own true self again," he murmured. "And I need not blush to meet my old grandfather's eye, and own myself a true and honest Norseman."

"And as for that incipient love affair," he added mentally, "I am glad that it is all over, and that Fate was wiser than I."

The minute hand of the Cathedral clock was was fast approaching twelve; Varberg reluctantly tore himself loose from the spell of contemplation, and entered the church through the middle portal. A large crowd of people had gathered about the famous astronomical clock, awaiting the appearance of Christ and his twelve apostles. Varberg hurried up the aisle, regardless of the worshippers, who knelt solitary or in scattered groups about the shrine of some cherished saint, and he succeeded in elbowing his way through the crowd, and in gaining a favorable position among the first rows of the spectators. Inside the railing a Frenchman, in a semi-clerical attire, and, somehow or other, with the appearance of a degraded ecclesiastic, stood violently gesticulating, as he pointed out and described the numerous complications of this eighth wonder of the world. As the hour of noon arrived, and all were breathlessly expectant, the throng became denser about the railing, and everybody stood on tiptoe, endeavoring to look over his neighbor's head. The hush became intenser; the Frenchman raised his hand solemnly; Varberg bent forward, and saw—two deep dark eyes glowing upon him. In the same instant there came a surprised "Oh." All heads were swiftly turned, but fortunately then the Four Ages of Man gave the signal, and struck the four quarters of the hour. But Olaf—what did he heed the Four Ages? The old skeleton, Father Time, struck twelve blows on his bell, the angel on the first gallery jingled on his instrument, and the twelve apostles moved out and made an abrupt bow before the figure of the Saviour; but on Olaf's senses all these musical noises buzzed and hummed remotely, like the rush of distant waters. He desperately clung to the possibility of a delusion, but soon the uncertainty culminated in the conviction that these eyes could belong to none other than Ruth; he looked once more—there was no room for doubt; it was Ruth. While the clock still kept up its noise, he strove hard to collect his thoughts; Ruth had again turned her head, and was apparently absorbed in the miraculous mechanism. The cock flapped his wings, and crowed thrice, and a chorus of ghostly echoes answered from the remotest recesses of the church. There was something shudderingly gay in this shrill metallic voice, which struck mockingly against the solemn vaults, then as it were suddenly froze, dropping down dead or vanishing in mid air. It reminded Varberg of the sensation he had had when entering the Chamber of Horrors in Mme. Toussaud's wax-works in London. As the people began to disperse, and the old Frenchman prepared to draw the curtain before the clock, he advanced a step, and stood at Ruth's side.

"There *is* evidently a destiny which shapes our ends, Miss Copley," said he, holding out his hand to her. "I am so mystified that I almost shudder, both with surprise and pleasure."

"You say that you are pleased to see me, Mr. Varberg," answered she, with a strange questioning glance in her eye, "but I must confess you *look* anything but pleased. Now what shall I choose to believe? your words or your face?"

"I thought we knew each other too well to misinterpret each other's faces in that way," replied Olaf, and attempted to smile. "If I should in this moment accept the testimony of your own face, I should reach anything but a flattering conclusion. But—by the way, where are your aunt and your cousin?"

"Dearie is here in the church somewhere, but aunt was too tired to go; she hasn't been quite well since we left Leipsic, and I suppose we shall have to stay here for a few days, until she is rested."

Side by side they walked down the aisle, asking and answering such indifferent questions as spontaneously fall from the lips when people meet after a brief separation. Ruth was provoked with herself for having given utterance to her surprise at seeing him; and she was half angry with him for having made no such betrayal of his feelings.

"He didn't even come to tell me good-by, although he had promised to do so," she thought. "Now I shall do my best to show how little I care." And she went on constructing ingeniously revengeful plans against Varberg, of how she would snub and ignore him, so as to remove the impression which she feared that her late efforts in his behalf must have given him; but at the bottom of her heart there lurked a dread, which almost amounted to a conviction, that he had it in his power to frustrate all her fierce resolutions. In her present revengeful mood, however, she was loath to confess to any such weakness, and she persevered in plotting, until she grew almost cheerful in the contemplation of her own shrewd devices.

"Miss Copley," began he at last in a low voice, as they stopped before the sculptured monument of the Bishop of Lichtenberg, "I have as yet had no opportunity to thank you for your—"

"Pray don't," she interrupted him hastily. "You have nothing to thank me for. What I did was nothing but my simple duty—a duty to myself rather than to you."

"Ah," he muttered sadly, as he fixed a grave reproachful glance upon her. "I understand. You need have no fear, however, of my misinterpreting your motives. I know you too well to suspect you of sentimentality, and if I was bold to infer that a friendly regard for me prompted your action, then I beg a hundred times your forgiveness. I promise you, I shall never think so again."

She saw in a moment that she had cruelly misjudged him; that she had been selfish and ungenerous; but she was not in a humor to make any such confession, and she forcibly banished the unwelcome thought, shook her head impatiently, and said, "Mr. Varberg, what makes you so stupid to-day? You didn't use to be so before. Why not talk about something more cheerful? It can do us no good to dwell upon that which is past. What is done cannot be helped."

He was about to answer; but just then they were discovered by Miss Bailey, who, quite forgetful of where she was, came running toward them, seized Varberg's hand, and exclaimed, "Why, Mr. Varberg, who in the world would have expected to find you here? How delightful that you have come. Both Ruth and I have been very much in need of a gentleman to take us around, and we have been wishing a million times that you were here."

Ruth scowled and pinched her cousin in the arm; but innocent Dearie, not understanding the hint, tore her arm loose, and cried out, "But, Ruth, why do you pinch me?" The situation was truly embarrassing; Varberg hastened to inquire more particularly after Mrs. Elder's health, and Dearie answered with a circumstantial account of their movements since they had left Leipsic.

"I thought you were going directly to England," said he, in order to say something.

"So we were," replied Dearie, while they followed Ruth, who was hastily approaching the door. "But Ruth had taken it into her head that she wanted to see the Saxon Switzerland, and so we went to Dresden and stayed a few days in the mountains. Now we are going from here to Paris, and then to London; and we expect to spend the summer with some relatives of ours in Northumberland."

As they reached the street Ruth again joined them, but she left to Dearie and Varberg to carry on the conversation, and only now and then threw in an indifferent remark. She carried her head proudly, and in his eyes she looked even taller and more queenly than usual; but he noticed a burning red spot upon her pale cheek, and the restlessness of her glance betrayed her inward agitation. At the door of Hotel de Paris they stopped. Dearie urged him to come in and dine with them, but he politely refused.

"But aunt would be so glad to see you."

"I shall have the pleasure of calling upon her before leaving the city."

"Then we shall expect you this afternoon. You will be sure to come, won't you?"

"Certainly."

For more than two hours he loitered leisurely about the city, listening for awhile to the military band which played in the Place d'Armes, criticising the statues of Guttenberg and Marshal Saxe, and indulging in philosophical reveries at the sight of the desolation which the late siege has left behind it. No friendly ivy drapes the nudity of these fire-blackened ruins of the Neu-Kirche and the great Municipal Library, and time has not yet softened those sharp broken lines into anything like picturesqueness and pathetic harmony. Masses of *débris* still lie undisturbed in the angles of the court, and the black walls, in melancholy defiance, loom up against the clear blue sky. Varberg was the more impressed by all that he saw because, in his present mood, a sad spectacle had a profounder significance to him than a cheerful one. He would gladly have persuaded himself that Ruth's conduct was a matter of indifference to him; and when at length he was forced to face the truth, he vainly attempted to put a humorous interpretation upon it, and ended with pitilessly deriding himself for his cowardly dependence upon a woman's whims.

The Inn of the Holy Ghost lives on the memory of Goethe, as indeed many other second-rate hotels on the continent do. The company which Varberg met at the *table d'hôte* was not by any means select; but to his surprise he found it almost exclusively French, and little keenness of insight was required to discover, that the Teutonic language grated on Gallic ears. He concluded from the frown of the little gentleman opposite, with the martial moustache and the threadbare coat, that there was some mistake prevailing in regard to his nationality; and in order to remove the unfavorable impression, he took pains to address the waiter in French. But the little gentleman's frown grew fiercer, and a half-bucolic individual, who sat dozing over a plate of fruit and a bottle of wine, suddenly waked up, quaffed his last glass at one draught, and rose from the table. The waiters brought the dinner, and Varberg fell to eating; and the Frenchman, to whom silence was even more repugnant than the Germans, gradually relented, bent over toward the stranger, and asked, "Is this the first time you visit France, sir?"

Varberg replied that it was.

"Then," continued the little man, who probably was ignorant of the Treaty of Versailles and the removal of the boundary, "there is a great pleasure in store for you. This country is even more beautiful than Italy, and I have been there too."

"You say *this country*," remarked Olaf; "do you mean France or Germany?"

A tremendous scowl darkened the face of the Gaul, and his eyes seeemed to shoot sparks.

"Are you a German, sir?" he cried.

"I am not."

"What are you then, if I may ask?"

Varberg had to debate the question before answering. Hitherto he had always called himself a Norwegian, but he felt no longer his former pride in the name. The memory of his old grandfather shot through his brain; then came the alluring thought of Ruth, and it seemed as if the two were irreconcilable opponents who fought for the possession of his heart. A treacherous blush burned on his cheek, and after a moment's reflection he said, "I am an American." And to drown the voice of conscience he emptied a glass of Rhenish.

Again Ruth had conquered.

CHAPTER XI.

The Cathedral Tower.

IT was about five o'clock in the afternoon when Varberg handed his card to a waiter in Hotel de Paris, with the request that it should be carried to Mrs. Elder. In the meanwhile he was shown into a reading room, where, quite unexpectedly, he found Ruth seated at a table, apparently absorbed in a German newspaper. Her recent agitation had left no trace behind; she seemed as cheerful and unconcerned as if nothing had happened. As she caught sight of Varberg she arose from her seat, came toward him and offered him her hand in her own easy, natural way.

"Ah, I am glad you did not play the truant again," said she laughing as she gave him a place at her side on the sofa. "By the way, what horribly stupid things these foreign newspapers are. I have been trying to amuse myself with the 'Kölnische Zeitung,' but I find it a very dreary sort of business. Not even an interesting obituary notice."

"Then you read obituary notices for amusement?" remarked he with a little show of surprise.

"Well, call it what you please," answered she carelessly. "They are always the first thing I read in a newspaper. And now, tell me honestly, don't *you*, too, feel just a little bit disappointed when you glance through an obituary column and don't find a single name you know in it?"

She asked the question with such evident sincerity that he couldn't help laughing.

"Well, yes, when I think of it," he said, "I must confess that I have had a similar sensation. However, as regards the German newspapers, you are hardly just when you say that they are dull because they don't interest you."

"Oh, yes, I am perfectly just. I have talked with German ladies about it, and they say that they never find the papers worth reading; and at home I should be just as likely to forget to eat my breakfast as to omit reading the morning paper."

At this moment the servant announced that Mrs. Elder was ready to receive Mr. Varberg, and both mounted the stairs together. On the way he revolved in his mind what could have wrought this sudden change in Ruth, and he hastily recalled the words which had passed between them in the morning, vainly seeking a clue to the mystery.

"I should like to know," reflected he, "what sort of introverted logic it is which governs her mental machinery. And, after all," he added, as she opened the door to him, "what would be the good of it? If I could comprehend her, I should probably not find her half so delightful. I must accept her as I accept a miracle, and the fairest miracle which God ever wrought."

He found Mrs. Elder seated in a large easy-chair and propped up in pillows. She was amiable, placid, and exhaustive as usual.

"How happy you ought to be, Mr. Varberg," said she, after having languidly expressed her delight at seeing him, "who are going to a country of snow and glaciers, while we shall have to languish here in this insufferable heat."

To Mrs. Elder's obstinate fancy, Norway was,

even at midsummer, an interminable Arctic snow field. She had evidently not profited by the Norseman's teachings, and on this occasion he meekly coincided with her, and gave up all further attempts at conversion.

"We have just been spending some time in Dresden," resumed the old lady after a brief silence, "and we have been very much delighted with the galleries. But we should have enjoyed them more if we had had you to explain the pictures to us."

"No, with your permission, aunt," Ruth interposed, "I shall have to object to that. You will forgive me, Mr. Varberg, if I say that I, at least, enjoyed the galleries the better for being alone. An art critic like yourself may be a very valuable *cicerone* for one who travels for instruction. But I only went to have a pleasant time; and in your presence I should never have dared to pass my irreverential criticism upon all those stilted saints and martyrs, and they in return would not have had the courage to take me into their confidence, and discourse with me humanly and show me their humorous as well as their official and pious side. With your keen eye passing judgment upon them, they would have been simply grave and graceful and—decorous."

"I was not aware," replied Varberg laughing, "that my humble presence could be so awe-inspiring."

"Oh yes, Mr. Varberg, you know you disapprove of jokes, and even saints are not always deficient in humor."

"Well, if you say so, I will try to believe that you are right. But then you must favor me with a specimen of your criticism; perhaps I am not so lacking in appreciation as you think. What is your opinion, say, of the Holbein Madonna?"

"Well, she is not humorous, I admit. But I read more of motherly sadness than of motherly pride in her countenance. That sickly looking child evidently belongs to those homely, Dutchy looking Burgomaster folks who are kneeling in the foreground. The prim apostles of Raphael and his clique, with their graceful attitudes and their faultless draperies, I enjoyed thoroughly. I imagined myself running a pin into their arms or tumbling their curls, and I wondered if they would then know how to preserve their studied dignity. The roasting saints of Ribera and Velasquez I also grew very fond of, and as for the Dutch nymphs, and fawns, and peasants, their humor is as broad as the daylight, and there is no need of straining the interpretation."

"If you have nothing worse to report," said he, "then on my own account, I sincerely regret my absence. You might have taught me many a useful lesson, and opened my eyes to things which I should never have discovered of my own accord."

"Oh, no, I should only have horrified you by admiring the wrong thing, and I should have lost fifty per cent. in your estimation."

Mrs. Elder and Dearie now related their experiences, and the conversation took another turn. After half an hour's talk, Varberg invited the ladies to accompany him on a walk through the city; but Dearie declared she could not leave her aunt, and so the end of it was that Ruth and Varberg went alone.

Strasbourg, even in its gayest holiday attire, wears an aspect of idyllic drowsiness. It is not an aspiring city. All its grandeur lies in the past; it wears upon its brow an habitual air of mystery, and its romantic suggestiveness will yield to the gentlest touch of fancy; and then it lapses into a profound reverie, from which not even the rough voice of the nineteenth century can rouse it. This was in brief the substance of Varberg's remarks, as he walked with Ruth through the narrow street which leads from the Kleber Platz up to the Cathedral. She listened for awhile patiently, but at last she looked almost imploringly at him and said, " Now please, don't let us be profound. You take a peculiar pleasure in going beyond my depth, but this time I shan't let you. By the way, do you remember the young lady with the yellow hair whom I told you to talk nonsense to at the ball in Leipsic."

" Of course I remember her."

" Well, that time you succeeded admirably. She confessed to me the next day that she thought you were the brightest man she had ever met with. In fact, she was half in love with you. I know it is unkind in me to tell you of it, but you will probably never see her again, so it makes no difference, Now, why do you reserve all your brightness for others, and vent all your learning on poor me?"

"Miss Ruth, you are incorrigible," he broke forth, looking pleased rather in spite of himself. "You needn't say, however, that I am going beyond your depth, for your own answers contradict you. I might rather turn your accusation against yourself. I never know what you are going to do or say next. Indeed, you are a perpetual puzzle to me."

"Then you ought to feel thankful, Mr. Varberg," retorted she with that arch look of hers, "that you have at last found something which you don't understand."

"To understand a woman, and especially you! What a presumption! I should as soon undertake to square the circle."

"That is well enough to say," she answered. "But apropos of Strasbourg: you have praised this city so much that I feel like abusing it. Tell me, would you really like to live here? Don't you think that everything looks insufferably sleepy?"

"What you call sleepiness is the very thing which delights me. This vague mediæval glamour which still hangs brooding over this colossal tomb of history softens the voice and muffles the footfall of the noisy life of to-day—"

"Wait one moment!" cried Ruth. "You are scattering pearls to the winds. Wait, till I can get my note-book."

"Only look at our own cities," continued Varberg, without heeding the interruption, "and the contrast cannot but strike you. Take, for instance, New York, or even your much cherished Boston, and artistically speaking, what is there to it? A rigidly formal, monotonous heap of brick and mortar, pitilessly new, glaringly angular, wide awake, and unrelieved by any suggestion of sentiment, poetry, or romance."

"What an outrage!" exclaimed she, and stopped abruptly in the street. "Remember, I was born in Boston, and am as loyal to my country as you are to Strasbourg. If a man could live on picturesqueness, I should find it reasonable enough that you prefer this musty old nest to a bright, wide-awake New England town. If I were the magistrate of Strasbourg," she added jocosely, "I think I should order a semi-annual bombardment only to rouse the inhabitants from their torpor. With us we have at least an occasional murder, or an elopement, or at all events, a run-away team, to enliven the public sentiment; but it seems that even the horses here are too decorous to indulge in any sort of frivolity."

They stood on the square before the cathedral, and the combative spirit died out in the minds of both. It seemed no longer the same church they had seen in the morning. In the broad light of the noon it wore an air of epic grandeur and repose; now the intenser mood of the evening had quickened its stone pulses with a new life, and with grand lyrical impulse the huge labyrinthine texture of arch, buttress, and tracery started up into the red, faintly-flushed sky. The colossal façade, bathed in the deep-tinged gold of the late sun, lent by its contrast a touch of terror to the massive gloom which filled the recesses of the eastern buttresses.

"That man's name was not 'writ in water,'" remarked Ruth, "who built this church as an epitaph on himself."

"It is not the epitaph of a man," replied Varberg, "but the monument of ten generations."

"What a pity that the south tower is wanting,

and that the present spire, somehow or other, refuses to carry out the noble purpose of the façade. That florid and fantastic style of the fifteenth century—"

His features must have betrayed his astonishment, and Ruth, seeing his comically perplexed look, could no longer retain her composure, but burst out into ringing laughter.

"Oh," she cried, "you are the easiest man to impose upon that I ever knew. I read it all in Baedeker this morning, and I thought I would like to try it on you, just to see how you would take it."

"Well, and what is the result of your experiment?" asked Varberg, joining in her laughter, because he felt that it was expected of him. "However, next time when you may wish to impose upon me, I should advise you to choose a less accessible source than Baedeker."

"Now, don't be exasperating, if you please;" and Ruth, as if quite by accident, laid her arm in his and looked up into his face in the most bewitching manner. What was there in that look which chased the blood to his cheeks, and made his pulses quicken? "Did he misunderstand me? Is he offended with me?" was all it seemed to say; but to him it carried a far profounder meaning. It revealed to him his own utter helplessness in the grasp of the passion which had so mercilessly clutched at the very roots of his heart. He felt himself as the victim of some fatal destiny, which with cruel joy calmly frustrated every plan and purpose of his life. And all the while he stood with a distracted smile about his lips; but his eyes were sad, and a gathering gloom clouded his brow. The interrogation marks in Ruth's eyes grew until at last she broke forth in a voice of alarm: "But, Mr. Varberg, you are not really angry with me, are you?"

"Ah, Miss Ruth," he murmured vacantly; "I angry with you? I wish I could be angry with you. I should be a happier man if I could."

"Yes, I know you like to mystify me," she answered musingly; and then, as if trying to banish the importunate thought which his words suggested, she added in a merrier tone, "And this time I ought to confess that you have succeeded admirably."

At this moment an old French guide half

timidly approached them, and in a husky, sepulchral voice offered to conduct them through the church and up into the tower. He had a most pathetic air of shabbiness and humiliation, as if he had been doomed to bear upon his shoulders all the burden and disgrace of the late war. An ex-military coat of uncertain color hung loosely about his limbs, and his moustache had a decided shade of green, like a certain kind of moss which grows upon the branches of the pine. Indeed, as Ruth remarked, he was a most pathetic character, and she was at once prepossessed in his favor. As they passed under the wide portal, he began to tell them the old story of Erwin of Steinbach, the architect of the façade, and his lovely daughter Sabina; but Ruth interrupted him, saying that she knew as much about them as he did. The disconcerted guide then humbly called their attention to the carved stone statues which adorned the niches of the side portals.

"It is the twelve foolish virgins," he said.

"The twelve foolish virgins!" exclaimed Ruth. "Were they all twelve foolish? Besides, I did not know that there were more than ten of them."

"The twelve foolish virgins," repeated the guide meekly.

"That man is a genuine pessimist," said she, in English, turning to Varberg. "He has even less confidence in the sex than you have. He must have been cruelly jilted."

"I should call that rather a rash conclusion," answered he. "You think, then, that pessimism is the natural result of blighted hopes."

"Usually it is. And still I do not deny that there are those who are born pessimists."

They entered the church and walked up the full length of the nave, to a side chapel where a tonsured priest had gathered a small flock of the faithful, to whom he was delivering a half-humorous discourse on the life and character of St. Joseph. This man of God had been neglected of late, he said, but it was a great mistake; for he was a most helpful and efficient saint.

There is at all times a potent fascination about these miracles in stone, which we call Gothic cathedrals. But on a summer night, when the sun, in its downward course, pours a quivering stream of splendor through the windows of combined amethyst, topaz, and rose, when the air burns with all the deepest tinges of a tenfold intensified rainbow, and the gloom, with a dim suffusion of color, hovers indistinctly remote under the arched vaults overhead, then nature finishes in its own perfect spirit what the builders have left undone, and effaces the boundary line between the human and the divine.

"Somebody has said that the Gothic architecture is a divine revelation," whispered Ruth as, leaning on Varberg's arm, she moved down the south aisle. "Do you remember who said it?"

"I think it is Ruskin."

"To be sure, so it is. I think I now understand what he means. I admit too that on our side of the ocean we don't know what a church is. Our domestic little coops, with carpeted floor and a velvet-cushioned sofa for the minister to sprawl on, may do well enough for a social chat and a tea meeting, but they are hardly fit for worship. A place like this doesn't invite to familiarity. A tea-meeting here would strike even the rigidest Down East Puritan as absurdly incongruous, if not sacrilegious."

"I suppose our churches are the logical results of our republicanism," answered Varberg. "We like to be on familiar terms with God as with every one else."

"Perhaps," murmured Ruth absently, and gazed up to the great sun-illumined windows. Heavy drops of deep crimson, blue, and golden light grazed the clustered shafts of the columns, thrilling the dead stone into a brief blush of life.

"How beautiful," said she, "and still how sad! I should turn Catholic within a year, if I were doomed to visit this church daily."

The guide ventured to remind them, that if they wished to visit the tower, there was no time to be lost. At Varberg's suggestion, a little sallow-faced sacristan opened a small door in the transept, and let them out only a few steps from the entrance to the tower. The ascent was rather a laborious one, and before they had mounted the three hundred and thirtieth step, Ruth had at least ten times regretted her rash resolution into which, as she insisted, her friend had craftily beguiled her. Although he knew himself innocent of any such intent, he had had too long an experience to think of contradicting her; he only rendered her every possible assistance, reflecting all the while that the very helplessness of a beautiful woman makes her tenfold dear and lovable. Having inspected the great bell, and borrowed a stool at the warden's lodge, they hastened out on the platform; then as by a common impulse came to a sudden stop, and let their eyes range out over the magnificent landscape, spread out before them.

"Isn't it grand?" exlaimed Ruth ecstatically.

"If I only could forgive myself," began Varberg, with a malicious twinkle in his eye, "for beguiling you—"

"Now don't be preposterous," she demanded imperiously; and as if it were he who had made a martyr of himself, she turned a beaming countenance upon him, and added triumphantly, "Now don't you feel paid for your trouble?"

"Yes," he added, hardly able to restrain his laughter, "I feel under infinite obligation to you."

"Oh," she cried, with an impatient toss of her head, "how provoking you can be!"

He placed the stool near the railing on the unfinished southern tower, and she sat down.

Eastward toward Germany, the Black Forest region, made immortal by Auerbach's tales, lay steeped in purple gloom, and the broad plains of Lorraine glowed with the warm hazy light of the evening. Toward the north and west the chain of the Vosges stood dimly blue and ethereal, and closing the view toward the south, the sun-flushed peaks of the Jura traced themselves faintly upon the far horizon, glimmering with the airiest tints of delicate crimson and rose. On the square below, men moved about like little black spots, and the sombre, steep-roofed houses, with the stork's nest under the masoned chimney, sent forth feeble columns of smoke which rose lazily and vanished into the thin air. Varberg read with the profoundest reverence the name of Goethe, carved by the poet himself in the stone while he was a student in the University of Strasbourg. Ruth as usual could not summon any sentiment at the sight of that name, and remained provokingly cold while her companion improvised a little eulogy.

"Tell me, Miss Ruth," he said at last, "what is your reason for disliking Goethe so much?"

"Well," she answered emphatically, "he wasn't a good man."

Now Varberg had not forgotten that hardly three weeks ago Ruth had declared to him that she hated good young men, and he was greatly tempted to remind her of it; but he had long ago ceased to wonder at the contradictions in her character; he merely accepted them as psychological facts, which he stored in his mind for future use. Goethe had done the same, and very likely that was the very reason why she hated him.

"Goethe was not a good man," remarked Olaf, "and therefore you dislike him as an author."

"Of course," she replied, with an air as if that was the most natural thing in the world.

The setting sun now kindled the western sky with a great blaze of color; the windows of the houses on the opposite side of the square burned with its fiery reflection, and the huge shadow of the cathedral, visibly lengthening, moved slowly eastward shrouding the street in deepening glamour. Varberg seated himself on the battlement of the tower, and while Ruth was apparently absorbed in the sunset, stole frequent glimpses of her fair young features. They both yielded to the magic of the situation, and unconsciously lapsed into silence. The strangeness of the scene—the vast stillness, and the deep-toned richness of the evening—imperceptibly wrought upon their senses and soothed the noisier impulses of their hearts; a feeling of sympathy and mutual understanding stole over them; their eyes met with a quick response, and a smile, more eloquent than words, reassured both that the last film of the cloud which had during the day had been hovering between them was at length dispersed. Thus it happened that in those brief moments he dared to face the resolution which in spite of misgivings, counterplots, and his own wish to the contrary, he had dimly foreseen as the inevitable end of their acquaintance. "It is no whim or fancy," he said to himself; "it is a passion, interwoven with the very fibres of my soul. It is useless to strive against the current." And with a composure which would have appeared preposterous to himself, had he thought of viewing it objectively, he matured step by step the later movements of the campaign, and weighed the chances of failure or success as coolly as if it had been the fate of some helpless stranger which had been submitted to his disinterested decision. He would not propose to Ruth at once, partly because he wished to gain time, partly because he was by no means convinced that she loved him. Indeed, it seemed such an absurd thing that any woman should love him, that he was more likely to reach a negative conclusion. In the meanwhile he would try to induce her to pay a visit to Norway, then invite her to spend a month or so in his grandfather's house, and if their relation continued to develop in the same direction as heretofore, the climax would be inevitable. But what could Ruth be thinking about, as she sat there, smiling to herself with that look of profound abstraction in her eyes? Evidently the sunset was no longer occupying her attention. Perhaps she involuntarily answered this mental question by the remark she made.

"After all, I think you are a very good American, Mr. Varberg," she said, as if taking up the thread of a conversation dropped only a minute before. " In spite of all your admiration of the old world, you show plainly that in your heart of hearts your sympathy is with the new."

"To my mind, Miss Ruth," he answered with an energy which startled her, "the new world means you, and what a truism it would be to say that in this acceptation the new world is dearer to me than the old."

He hardly realized that he was on the verge of a declaration; but Ruth felt it, and she grew visibly uneasy. With a sudden jerk she thrust the end of her parasol into a little hole in the battlement, and began assiduously to dig out the gravel; then she discovered some object down on the square which for the moment absorbed all her attention.

"What a queer bird the stork is," she said at last, with a cheery unconcern, which would have been a death-blow to his hopes had it not contrasted so absurdly with the agitation of her manner. Had she known, however, the association of ideas in his mind, she would hardly have made that remark about the stork. His knowledge of that bird had been derived from Hans Christian Andersen's stories.

"Yes," he replied, after a moment's hesitation, "the stork is a queer bird. It is the bird of happiness."

"The bird of happiness," she murmured, gazing vacantly out into the blue space.

"Pardon me, *monsieur*," said a creaking voice close to Varberg's ear; "but it is time to close the church." There stood the shabby little guide, with his cap in his hand, and smiled and bowed deferentially. Ruth and Varberg rose, gave one long look of farewell to the magnificent landscape, and began their descent in silence. Having reached the street, they dismissed the guide, who gave them as a souvenir a picture of four pigs, which, when folded up, represented the likeness of the third Napoleon.

"You are evidently not an admirer of the ex-Emperor," remarked Varberg.

"The Emperor? God bless him!" replied the old man pathetically. "The other guides all have this picture, and I must do what the rest do. *Monsieur*," he added in a tone of inexpressible sadness, "I was born in this city, and I have not the money to go away." And he wagged his head and shuffled along, while the wooden heels of his shoes clattered mournfully against the pavement.

They had intended to go directly to the hotel, but for some reason or other they did not do it. For more than an hour they wandered about on the ramparts of the city, conscious all the while of a latent excitement which, as they half expected, might at any moment break the frail bonds of conventionalism. Ruth was not at all sure that she desired it; perhaps if she had put the question boldly to herself, she would have decided that she positively dreaded it. But she was enough of a woman to love excitement for its own sake; and as she did not feel it incumbent upon her to solve the problem one way or the other, she simply yielded to the fascination which the very uncertainty exerted over her, and allowed herself to drift onward with the fluctuating emotions of the moment, regardless of whither they carried her. In fact, they were both in that delightfully impersonal mood which men are too apt to indulge when in novel or absurd situations. Varberg, in the meanwhile, had framed at least twenty resolutions in regard to the decisive question of

Ruth's visit to Norway; but he felt that much depended upon the shape in which it was put, and although an accomplished linguist, he could find no phrase worthy of embodying so serious a sentiment. It was after nine o'clock when they reached her hotel, and he had not yet spoken. He accompanied her through the vestibule to the foot of the staircase, where with fluttering hearts, they both paused and gazed expectantly into each other's faces.

"Miss Ruth," he said at last, holding her hand in his, "I have one thing to ask of you. Will you come and visit my home this summer, and take Mrs. Elder and Dearie with you? My grandparents and all of us would be so happy to see you."

She hesitated, dropped her eyes, and again suddenly raising them, she said firmly, "I will."

"Is it a promise?"

"It is." And she quickly withdrew her hand and ran up stairs.

The next morning Varberg took the train for Paris. Four days later he landed in London, and within a week boarded the steamer which was to carry him to the land of his birth.

CHAPTER XII.

The Land of the Vikings.

IT was in the last days of July. Olaf had hastened away from Bergen, where the English boat had landed him, had boarded a Norwegian steamer, and saw now from afar the blue snow-peaked mountains which guarded the entrance to the valley of his birth. The sky was one vast unruffled calm, the water glittered with cool green and emerald reflections, and overhead and far down in the deep the white clouds floated airily through a limitless expanse of blue. The young exile stood in the prow of the steamer, and his heart throbbed as if it longed to burst his bosom. His senses were keenly awake; every passing object, every fresh memory traced its impressions clearly upon his mind, and produced a quick succession of varying emotions. It was as if this pure, bracing mountain air had penetrated into his very soul, and was stimulating the slumbering energies of his nature. And still—he could not but own it—he was no longer that fresh, trusting, primitive youth who, five years ago, started out from his mountain home to conquer an unknown happiness in the world beyond the sea. Would he now be capable of making the sacrifice to which he had then so cheerfully submitted? He knew that he would not. Even at this moment he feared that the emotion he experienced was half spurious; he had never been more bewilderingly conscious of the duality of his nature, and the contrast between the warm-blooded impetuosity of the youth who departed and the more consciously self-critical mood of the man who returned, was not altogether imaginary. During these many years spent among strangers, he had had no experiences which had really stirred the depths of his heart, and he had accordingly imagined that he had lost the power of loving. Then came Ruth with all the wealth of her deep, womanly nature, which she shielded beneath the appearance of light-hearted skepticism and caprice; in her he had, as she herself expressed it, found something which he did not understand,

and after having vainly striven to reduce her to logic, he had abandoned the attempt and loved her instead.

"Would she understand this Norseland home of mine?" he asked himself; "would she love it as I do?"

The steamer now cleared a steep headland; Varberg held his breath, then gave a shout, and sprang up on the bridge. There, on the green slope, close to the water, a white, stately mansion peeped forth from behind its dense screen of foliage, and beckoned to him with a grave, familiar eye of gentle reproach and welcome. As soon as the steamer came into view, a large flag flew up on the flag-pole at the point of the pier, and a row of cannon stationed along the beach boomed forth a joyous salute, which rolled away over the surface of the water, and lost itself in tumultuous echoes among the distant peaks of the glaciers. It revealed such a vast perspective of sound as almost to bewilder the sense with its suggestion of limitless space and power. It was to Varberg as if the very mountains were calling to him with their granite voices, and sending him from afar their stern greeting. They had watched over him from his birth up, and had sung their stormy lullabies at his cradle; the ever-watchful eye of their glaciers had witnessed his boyish sports; many a silent summer night the pine woods had told him their sombre legends, and the cataracts in quivering whispers of spray had confided to him their tenderest memories. Now, in one quick flash, his whole past life spread out before him, and he saw, perhaps for the first time in his life, what he had renounced.

The steam whistle sounded thrice, and a white-painted shallop (the same shallop which once he had called his own) was thrust out from the pier. In the stern stood an old gray-haired man, and close to him sat a young girl with a light straw hat on her head, and a mass of blonde hair. There were two stalwart men at the oars, and the young lady held the tiller. It needed but a glance to convince Olaf that it was his old grandfather and Brynhild, his sister. The boat glided swiftly out over the glittering mirror of the fjord, the gentle ripple about its bow undulated in long, diverging lines over the glassy surface, and every stroke of the oar sent little throngs of eddying bubbles floating shoreward in its wake. Olaf stood intently watching all this, and it appeared to him like some magnificent chapter in a book, very beautiful, but absurdly unreal. He also noticed that red and white streamers were flying from the gables of the mansion, and that handkerchiefs were waving to him from the balcony, from the windows, and from the boat. The whistle sounded for the third time, the engine rumbled, and the wheels plashed and beat the water into a mass of seething foam. He then suddenly remembered where he was, tore off his hat, and waved his pocket-handkerchief. The gangway was lowered, and his grandfather, followed by Brynhild, sprang up the steps as if he had been a youth of twenty. Olaf leaped down from the bridge; then there was a scream, and the young girl flung her arms about his neck, and laughed and shed tears in an altogether irrational manner. He kissed her, but could not think of a word to say; then gently released himself and grasped the hand of his grandfather, who stood gazing at him with a look of mingled tenderness and surprise.

"My dear boy," he broke forth in a voice

which trembled with emotion, "God be praised that He has given you back to us again. But, to be sure, you have changed much."

"For the worse, do you think, grandfather?" said Olaf, summoning all the Norwegian which for the moment was at his command.

"Yes, indeed, for the worse," cried Brynhild, who was still clinging to her brother's arm and gazing at him with moist wide-opened eyes; "why have you allowed your beard to grow? You looked a great deal better as you were when you left home."

"I am sorry to hear it. However, I can hardly myself be held responsible for my looks. But how is grandmother?"

And now followed a perfect torrent of questions such as may be more readily imagined than told. The baggage was carried down into the boat, the smoke-stack rolled out dense volumes of smoke, and the slender escape-pipe behind it sent forth an abrupt, provoked shriek, and from sheer exhaustion lapsed into silence. Olaf helped his sister down into the shallop, old Mr. Varberg followed, and the oarsmen took their seats on the row benches. The sun shone brightly and poured a flood of splendor upon the glacier steeples; the smooth waters sparkled as if oversown with sunny jewels; the air was so inconceivably pure and transparent, the meadows lay so soft and green under the brow of the pine-covered cliffs, and every hill, every glen, every mountain was an old acquaintance, and hid in its stony breast an ore of golden memories. A sense of joy and blessedness thrilled through the young man's frame; he was once more at home, among those who knew and loved him. The first feeling of bewilderment had vanished; the author lay a thousand miles behind him; now the moment asserted its right, and the past years of exile faded away like the confused phantoms of a dream. On the pier he was met by the old servants of the family, who all thronged forward to shake hands with him and offer him their welcome. Some told him that he had grown tall and handsome, others that he looked very foreign, and others again that he had not changed at all.

"And is this our little Olaf whom I used to rock in my lap when he was a baby?" said a wrinkled little woman, in whom he recognized his old nurse.

"And do you remember the time when you cried for a whole day, and refused to eat, because they had killed your cow Rosyside?" asked the family milkmaid.

Yes, he well remembered that; and the good old soul was so touched that she shed tears. These and numerous other questions were asked and answered, while the company moved up through the garden to the vestibule, where Olaf's grandmother stood, impatiently awaiting his arrival. She kissed and embraced him, wept over him, and said that now she had found him, and he must never leave her again. The servants remained standing at the foot of the stairs, the men with their caps in their hands, and the women giving vent to their emotion in sighs, and wiping their eyes with their aprons. It was a scene which, in its simple impressiveness, touched the homeless heart of the young wanderer. What a contrast to the great noisy world beyond the sea! With his grandmother and his sister on his arm, he entered the great drawing-room, with its heavy red curtains, its strange tapestries, and its long rows of ancestral portraits. In the middle of the floor stood a large table, on which wine and home-made cakes were spread in liberal profusion. Old Judge Varberg called the servants in, poured wine into the glasses, and then stationed himself solemnly at the head of the table. He lifted his glass, and all the others followed his example; whereupon he delivered a brief speech of welcome, in which he ingeniously avoided every allusion to the cause of his grandson's departure, as well as to the country in which he had spent his years of exile. The toast was drunk, the grandmother added her " Amen " and the servants retired, having once more shaken hands with the young heir of the house.

It was still early in the forenoon; the sunshine glided stealthily in between the ample folds of the window curtains, and lay in long streaks and patches upon the uncarpeted floor.

The austere ancestors, with their powdered wigs and pigtails, their lace-embroidered coats and golden-hilted swords, looked solemnly down upon their degenerate descendant, and the prim ancestresses, in Arcadian costumes, and with shepherds' staves in their hands, sent him meaning glances of reproachful recognition.

"If you had lived in my time, I should have known how to manage you," the grand old gentleman with the gold-headed cane seemed to say. But the sweet-faced, timid little lady, who had once been his wife, and whom Olaf in his boyhood so often had pitied, gazed tenderly at him, as if to say, "Whatever you are, you are my own flesh and blood. If your mother had been alive, you would not have found it in your heart to leave her."

If the painter could be trusted, there must have been a singular disproportion between the two as regards bodily stature; for the old gentleman, although standing upon the earth, leaned himself comfortably on the top of a stone lighthouse, the lantern of which shed a feeble glimmer out upon the distant sea, while the wife, whose waist was as thin as that of a wasp, was seated in an easy-chair, the back of which loomed up far above her head. It was this particular Varberg who, some three hundred years ago, had obtained from the Danish government a monopoly for building light-houses on the western coast of Norway; and after that, he had lived like a little king in his fjord, sending out his cruisers along the shore, and exacting toll from all passing vessels. He had had a light-house engraved on his seal, and had invariably written his name, "Varberg of the Light-house." The present Judge Varberg, to whom nothing was more precious than the traditions of his family, had scrupulously preserved the title, while Olaf, to whom the democratic convictions of his father were no less sacred, had persisted in ignoring it.

But all thought of past dissensions and disagreements vanished from Olaf's mind as he sat there in the large, old-fashioned sofa, and listened to the anxious questions and tender assurances of those who in all the world were nearest and dearest to him. On his right and left side sat the old people, holding his hands in theirs, and at his feet Brynhild was seated on a cricket, gazing up into his face with large affectionate eyes. Such a feeling of rest and security he had not experienced in all his life, and if it had not been for Ruth, he thought, he would have been content to forget all his youthful ambitions, and to live and die here in peace.

"But, my dear boy," said the old man, whose features had assumed a look of concern whenever

Olaf had opened his mouth to speak, "you have not forgotten your mother tongue, I hope. You speak with English accent."

"I was not aware of that, grandfather," answered Olaf, "but you must remember that I have not once had occasion to speak my own language during these five years. It may appear incomprehensible to you, and many would even call it affectation; but my daily experience has taught me that our language, being the mere external clothing of our thought, will, as naturally as the thought itself, receive the impress and the coloring of the land in which we live. I should, therefore, find it as unnatural to speak Norwegian in America as, a week from now, I should call it absurd to speak English here. But something of my American self still clings to me, and my organs of speech, as well as every other part of my being, will show it, at least for a time."

"God forbid that it should be of long duration, my son," retorted the Judge earnestly, rose from the sofa, and went out of the room.

It now became evident to Olaf that his grandparents intentionally ignored that part of his life which he had spent abroad; that they were as bitterly opposed to the land of his adoption to-day as they had been five years ago; and that in spite of his own protestations, they took it for granted that he had now returned to repent of his wild career and to settle down in his home for the future, as a peaceful, conservative citizen.

They were no doubt ready enough to forgive him, because, as the Judge had previously expressed it, every young man had to sow his wild oats, and this way was probably no worse than a good many others. But Olaf did not admit the guilt, and consequently asked no forgiveness; nevertheless, his discovery made him very uncomfortable, not only because it would debar him from the comfort of real confidence, but perhaps rather because in the depth of his heart there lurked a half-acknowledged inclination to listen to the voice of prudence, to choke the unprofitable ideals, to yield and surrender.

Olaf's grandfather was a fine-looking old gentleman of middle stature, and about seventy years of age. He had a strong growth of white, curly hair, a broad and massive forehead, and a slightly aquiline nose. The clear gaze of his calm blue eyes, as well as the firm lines about his mouth, indicated a keen understanding and a strong will, with perhaps a suggestion of obstinacy; but those eyes, which were usually so calm and clear, were a truly Protean feature; for when the old gentleman played his violoncello, they seemed to grow deeper, softer, and tenderer; and as the music gathered strength and burst forth in triumphant strains of joy, they would shine and sparkle with singular brilliancy. On the whole, judging from his appearance, no one would have believed that Mr. Varberg was seventy years old; his figure was quite erect, and his motions were youthful and vigorous. His wife was a venerable matron, tall and robust, straight as a candle, and with a certain abruptness in her bearing and manner. To be sure, Time had dealt roughly with the beauty of which she had once been so proud, and the traces of age were clearly legible upon her wrinkled brow; but for all that she was still a handsome old lady, and she did the honors at her parties with as much dignity to-day as she had done twenty years ago. It is no rare thing to find that people who have lived in harmony together for half a century bear a marked resemblance to each other; at all events, in the case of Judge and Mrs. Varberg the observation had been frequently made. They of course laughed at it themselves as an absurdity; but even Olaf could not help noticing the same mixture of determination and tenderness in the features of both. Mrs. Varberg invariably wore a white lace cap with dark blue ribbons and a black silk gown.

When dinner was over, and coffee had been served, the Judge asked his grandson if he would not like to take a ride on horseback, to which the latter willingly consented. A few minutes later the horses were at the door, and the old man appeared on the stairs, with spurs and riding boots. Olaf, having quite forgotten his grandfather's little weaknesses thoughtlessly offered him his hand to help him into the saddle.

"Bah!" cried the Judge in a provoked voice, and gave the youth a gentle blow over his fingers; "what do you take me to be? Do you think I am in my dotage? Only see that you get yourself safely into the saddle, and leave me to take care of myself."

The Judge had always prided himself on his self-dependence, and did not like to be reminded of his age. He at times himself referred to his seventy years, but that was quite another matter. He had been very impatient with his physician when, three years ago, he had forbidden him to skate. It was all the sheerest nonsense, he said, but nevertheless he heeded the injunction.

The afternoon was bright and warm; the air was soft and the sky pensively serene. The breeze was fraught with the fragrance of birch and wild flowers, with just a perceptible admixture of the briny breath of the sea. For a while they rode in silence along the smooth road, which usually followed the capricious curves of the numerous bays, and at times made a straight cut across come jutting headland. Everywhere the broad slope from the mountains down to the fjord was carefully cultivated, and green meadow and pasture land alternated with waving fields, well-tended orchards, and stray patches of birch and alder groves.

"This river," said the Judge, pointing with his riding-whip to a white torrent which dashed down over a rocky incline, "separates my lands from those of our friend the Colonel. Our properties, if united, would make the fairest estate in the kingdom."

Olaf had nothing to say to this, but he grew very hot about his ears, and felt exceedingly uncomfortable. His grandfather's eyes rested so steadily on him, and he was aware that much depended upon the way he answered. Suddenly a bright idea struck him.

"Yes," he said, straightening himself up in the saddle; "it would make a very fine estate indeed. What a pity that the Colonel has not a son, who might have married Brynhild. That is, as far as I can see, the only way in which your wish might be accomplished."

The old man's countenance fell; but he knew that it would not be prudent to push the matter for the present. So he spurred his horse; Olaf followed his example, and they galloped on to the bridge.

"This bridge," began the Judge, as the hoof-beats of the horses clattered along the stone pavement, "was built by my great-grandfather, Olaf Varberg, who died in the year 1681. And the structure is just as good to-day as it was two hundred years ago."

"Yes, it appears to be an exceedingly well-built structure," remarked Olaf approvingly.

Five minutes later they drew rein at the gate of a large buff-colored mansion, which was half hid behind a cluster of huge chestnut trees.

"If you have no objection, why not go in and call upon your old friend the Colonel?" said the Judge quite *en passant*, as if the thing had just occurred to him in the moment.

"Aha," thought Olaf; "that was what the ride was for. The trap was skilfully laid, but the game is too old to be caught." And in answer to the question he added aloud, "I have no objection. It makes no difference to me whether I call on the Colonel to-day or some other time, since the call has to be made."

They rode into the yard, where a footman came to take charge of the horses. Another servant showed them into the parlor, where the old Colonel sat enveloped in a cloud of tobacco smoke, and with a heap of newspapers on the table before him.

"Why, good evening, neighbor," cried the host in a voice as if he were addressing a regiment. "Rare guests, to be sure, and a thousand times welcome!"

The Colonel, who was a large portly gentleman, rose with difficulty from his leather-cushioned easy chair, and hobbled toward the new-comers.

"Well, neighbor, how is the gout?" inquired the Judge.

"The gout, sir? Ah, pretty miserable—pretty miserable, my friend. Up and down, up and down, like a three-wheeled wagon. And this is your boy. Ah, yes, I think I recognize him. I heard of his arrival. Well, you young vagabond, you have come home at last, and decided to live like a sensible mortal. Ha, ha, ha! And how do you like it?"

The Colonel laughed immoderately, and gave Olaf's hand a shake which tingled through the marrow of his bones.

"Well, well," continued he, turning to the Judge, who had in the meanwhile taken a seat on the sofa; "boys will be boys. We all have our failings, and the wildest colts, it is said, make the best horses."

Olaf felt the ire rising within him; but he struggled hard to keep calm. It seemed as if everybody was determined to look upon him as a sort of prodigal son, as a reformed reprobate who needed the indulgence and forgiveness of of his friends. That he had toiled bravely and broken an honorable career for himself; that he felt a manly pride in his achievements, and meant to build upon the foundation he himself had laid—this no one seemed to suspect. And while he sat there listening to the patronizing remarks of this ancient chatterbox his indignation changed to pity. What did these benighted mortals, who had spent all their days in this remote corner of the world, where a new idea was as rare a thing as an eclipse of the sun—what did they know of the great life in which his lot was cast? what standard had they whereby to measure him, and what right had they to judge him? While Olaf was diverting himself with these and similar reflections, the door was gently opened, and a young lady entered the room. She wore a light summer dress which fell in stiff folds about her slender body. She had grown taller since he saw her last, and an expression of sweet, gentle sadness dwelt in her features. Her complexion was wonderfully clear; her rich, yellow hair was bound in a Grecian knot on the back of her head, and a pure, lily-like beauty breathed from her whole being. She first bowed to the Judge, and then advanced to the window where Olaf was sitting. He rose and shook hands with her.

"Ah, Olaf," she said in a hushed, gentle voice; "how kind in you that you came so soon to see us. Father and I half feared that you had forgotten us."

The young man murmured something about the delight he experienced at seeing her, but in his heart he felt guilty and miserable.

"And how large you have grown, Olaf," continued Thora, while her eyes dwelt with visible pleasure on his countenance. "America has not changed you so much as I feared it would. Brynhild and I have talked about you so often, and we both wondered how you would look when you came back."

It was a luxury to him to hear her speak. It was many a year since anybody had called him by his first name, and upon her lips it sounded so sweetly and so exquisitely beautiful.

"I am happy to know that some one has thought kindly of me, Thora," he answered "You don't know what a strange experience it is to come home after so long an absence. I am so bewildered that I can hardly collect my senses It all appears to me like a charming story, too beautiful to be true."

"I am glad that you do find it beautiful here," she replied, with a pensive smile, "for we feared that after having travelled so much and seen so many grand and beautiful things, you would think everything very plain and simple here in your old home. And we are all very plain people, you know, and we don't hear much about what is going on in the world. Father has told me all about the war in France, and about the advantages of the English constitution, but I know he talks to me about such things only because he has nobody else to talk to, and I am sure I find it very difficult to remember what he explains to me."

He could not help smiling at her naïveté; nevertheless her words, by their very simplicity, impressed him deeply. He had long ago made the acquaintance of such characters in books, but he had quite forgotten that they also existed in reality. Five years ago he had himself been too much a part of this primitive life to be able to view it objectively. Thora had then to him been a beautiful young girl, and nothing more; now, in the capacity of an author, he discovered a new side to her character, and she accordingly assumed a fresh importance in his eyes.

The call was prolonged until almost an hour had passed, and Olaf and Thora made rapid advances in each other's favor. The two old gentlemen in the meanwhile discussed the prospects of the crops, the situation of King Amadeo, and the defeat of the Ultramontanes in Germany; but at times they paused to exchange a meaning glance, while they watched the young couple at the window with an air of profound satisfaction. At length the horses were brought to the door, and the visitors reluctantly departed. On the homeward way hardly a word was spoken. But as they dismounted at the garden gate, the Judge laid his arm on his grandson's shoulder (by the way, a very unusual thing for him to do), and said, " Well, how do you like the Colonel's daughter?"

" She is a very beautiful girl," answered Olaf hastily.

Many strange thoughts whirled about in Olaf Varberg's head that night, as he retired to his rooms—those same rooms which had witnessed his early struggles and dreams in his happy student days. Everything was just as when he left it. His favorite authors still stood in the bookshelves as he had himself arranged them; the pictures hung in their old places upon the walls, and gazed upon him with a familiar air of recognition; the carved furniture, with the green damask covers, the large canopied bed, with its flowered curtains—all was unchanged; it was as if he had but yesterday stepped out of this room —as if these five years, with their manifold experiences, had been but an empty dream, a bewildered fancy. He had come here—he hardly knew why—perhaps to enjoy a few brief days of rest—and now he found himself involved in a new and hopeless struggle.

He flung himself down in an easy-chair; paper and ink lay before him on the table. With a sudden resolution, he seized the pen and wrote a long letter to Ruth.

"She must come," he murmured, as he sealed the envelope; "and for the rest, let me trust to fortune."

CHAPTER XIII.

Ruth's Arrival.

TWO weeks had passed since Olaf's arrival. They had been very quiet and uneventful weeks, but nevertheless fraught with strange and novel experiences. Olaf had come to the conclusion that he was in fact the most complex character that ever lived. Already while in Leipsic had he discovered that the man and the author in him were, so to speak, two distinct individuals whose interests frequently clashed; Varberg the man had fallen in love with Ruth, while Varberg the author had remained provokingly cold. Now, to still further complicate the problem, a fresh difficulty thrust itself upon his attention. He found that his American life had developed one side of his nature which here in Norway he was forced to ignore; and his old Norse self, which had slumbered so long, was now awakening and asserting its rights with renewed power.

The days dragged along slowly and deliciously, and nothing occurred to break their calm, idyllic monotony. So Olaf had time enough for self-contemplation; and with the introspective tendency peculiar to youth, he groped vaguely about in the labyrinthine recesses of his being, and, as I have said, ended with deciding that he was the most complicated phenomenon under the sun. What especially perplexed him was his relation to Thora. He saw her almost daily, rowed with her on the fjord, took long walks with her through the fragrant birch groves, and saw with secret alarm their relation growing day by day more dangerously intimate. He did not seek her, neither did she seek him; but through some fatality their paths would inevitably meet. He always felt his heart beat faster when he saw her lithe figure in the shimmering shadow of the leaves; and he was immediately transported into that impersonal, romantic mood in which the maddest words and deeds seem so perfectly natural as almost to be trite and commonplace. Olaf, whose head was constantly filled with possible plots for novels and dramas, at such times assumed to himself a certain heroic character; he hovered high above the paltry realities of life, and felt as irresponsible as if he had been the Grand Mogul himself. He did not love Thora —at all events not in the sense in which he loved Ruth; but for all that, he was frequently conscious of a mad desire to propose to her, not because he was vain or heartless enough to trifle with her affections, but only in order to act out the plot, and to carry out the illusion to its last consequences. The air was so soft and calm, the sun burned so ethereally remote upon the sky, the mountains stood so serenely gigantic in the azure distance, the maiden at his side was so bewilderingly fair, and the whole scene contrasted so gratefully with the tumult of life from which he had lately escaped, as utterly to remove it from the sphere of responsible reality. It was all a beautiful idyllic romance of which he was the hero and she the heroine, and in romances people always propose, and his romantic sense of duty tempted him to do the same. What Thora's emotions may have been, we are not authorized to say; for Olaf's journals contain no hint, and still less any decisive evidence. She was a dutiful daughter, and was probably aware that her father was not averse to a connection of the two families; but whether her admirer was anything more to her than that abstract possibility of a husband which any young man of his attainments might have been, will always remain a matter of doubt.

Olaf had told his grandparents that some American friends would be visiting Norway during the summer; they had showed him great kindness during his stay in Germany, he said, and he hoped that there would be no objection to his inviting them to spend a couple of weeks in his home. He well knew that his request would be willingly granted, and he had therefore had no scruples in anticipating the decision. The long-expected letter from Ruth arrived at last, and during the next week the otherwise so quiet household was in a flutter of expectation, and the position, character, and appearance of the American guests were the all-absorbing topic of conversation.

It was a dim, warm evening—an evening of

deepest repose. The sun hung low over the western mountain tops, and the horizon was flushed with a faint crimson tint which shaded imperceptibly into the upper regions of purer blue. The water was as grave and placid as only the fjords of Norway can be. The large flag drowsed on its pole at the end of the pier, and at Olaf's direction a man was stationed on the beach, ready to fire the cannon as soon as the steamer came into view. And the signal was given. The echo thundered away over the mountains, and the huge, black boat came ploughing a path of foam through the glittering billows. Olaf and Brynhild, with two oarsmen, rowed out to receive the visitors. On the bridge stood a tall young lady, with a light straw hat on her head, and a brightly-colored shawl thrown around her shoulders; she leaned over the railing and waved her handkerchief, and Olaf and his sister responded from the boat. There is no need of dwelling on the scene of reception; half an hour later Ruth and Mrs. Elder entered the large drawing-room, and Olaf was so proud and happy that he felt inclined to shout or commit some other breach of propriety. Dearie had decided to remain with her relatives in England. The host and the hostess cordially welcomed the guests at the door, and Brynhild, who could not tear her eyes away from Ruth's countenance, eagerly relieved the ladies of waterproofs, hats, and shawls.

"How beautiful she is," murmured she in her brother's ear, and he nodded and smiled triumphantly.

Mrs. Elder's features wore an air of mild defiance and perplexity. Only a week ago, when she had reluctantly yielded to Ruth's energetic persuasions and accepted Olaf's invitation, it had been a serious question with her whether they ought not to bring with them their own bedding, and a small supply of provisions; the worthy old lady had even, with a secret relish, anticipated the patronizing attitude she, as a woman of the world, was to assume toward the natives. Now, all these pleasant prospects were spoiled; and as all Mrs. Elder's mental processes were slow, it would necessarily take some time before she could find herself at her ease in this surprisingly novel situation. Having drunk the toast of welcome, the guests retired with Brynhild to their rooms, and appeared again in time for supper. The Judge, with not a little formality, offered his arm to Mrs. Elder, Olaf hastened to Ruth's side, and a young officer, who wrote in the Judge's office, followed with Brynhild.

"And what is your impression of Norway, madam?" asked old Mr. Varberg, having brought his lady to a seat at his side.

"Ah, you speak English," exclaimed Mrs. Elder. "I didn't know that the natives of Norway generally spoke English."

"No; the natives of Norway generally do not," said the Judge emphatically.

Ruth grew uneasy; she knew that her aunt was treading on dangerous ground; but Olaf came to the rescue.

"I have been thinking of what we can do to amuse our guests while they are staying with us," he said, addressing himself to his grandfather. "You know the resources of the place, as it is to-day, better than I do. What, for instance, would you propose for to-morrow?"

"If the ladies are good climbers, you might make an excursion to the glaciers."

All parties present evinced a vivid interest in

this proposition, and numerous plans were suggested. It was finally decided that the excursion should be put off for a week, until more visitors had arrived, and the Americans had exhausted the wonders of the immediate vicinity.

Olaf, for some reason or other, was in high spirits, and his good humor was of a contagious kind and soon communicated itself to all the rest. He beguiled Mrs. Elder into recounting the incidents of their journey through France and their sojourn in England, and craftily contrived to start his grandfather and Ruth on a musical discussion concerning the relative merits of the old Mozart and Beethoven and the new Chopin and Wagner schools. Ruth expressed her opinions clearly, and with a beautiful naturalness and ease which evidently startled the old gentleman more than he was willing to admit. He was not accustomed to hear women talk in that way; and although he thoroughly enjoyed this free exchange of opinions, he was old-fashioned enough to question whether he really approved of the thing in the abstract. The grandmother, down at the other end of the table, was positive that she did not; to be sure, she did not understand English, and could not judge Ruth by what she said; but seeing that she was brilliant and beautiful, she instinctively felt that her arrival must mean something; and that this young lady's influence over her grandson would not be favorable to her own intentions with him was self-evident. Her own ideas of American young ladyhood, derived mostly from the accounts of English travellers, had represented the fair sex of our land as masculine, forward, and unattractive, and with the generalizing tendency of the feminine mind, she had immediately concluded that Ruth, from an affectional point of view, was altogether harmless. Could it be possible, she argued, that her boy was purposely leading her astray when he spoke with such perfect coolness of extending their hospitality to these foreigners? And she had blindly credited his proposal to a certain manly pride which did not allow him to receive without giving in return, and perhaps to a very pardonable desire to display the ancient wealth and glory of his home.

When the meal was at an end the young people rose, and, according to old Norse custom, went up to the master and the mistress of the house, shook hands with them, and said *Tak for Maden* (Thanks for the food). Ruth immediately caught these words, walked up to the Judge and his wife, and held out her hand.

"*Tak for Maden,*" she said.

The Judge grasped her hand, shook it heartily, and looked immensely pleased. Olaf in the meanwhile stood looking hard at Ruth, to discover if the old roguish twinkle was not lurking in her eye; but he only saw an open pleasant smile, evidently provoked by her unsuccessful attempt at pronouncing the foreign words.

"Ah," thought Olaf, and rubbed his hands contentedly; "she will have grandfather in love with her before a week is past."

The sun was yet peeping above the horizon, and the daylight still lingered. The air was as warm as at midsummer. The old folks took their seats out on the balcony, and the Judge ordered cigars and the ingredients requisite for making toddy. And there he sat smoking, and at the same time carrying on rather a laborious conversation with Mrs. Elder, acting as interpreter between her and his wife. Brynhild was occupied with her household duties, and Ruth and Olaf had seized the opportunity to take a walk on the beach.

"And now, Miss Ruth," he said, as soon as they were alone, "you must tell me what you think of Norway."

"To be candid," answered Ruth, "I don't think at all. I find no time for thinking. I can only see and enjoy. I have had many strange notions about this remote sea-kingdom, which I imagined to be your home, but my conjectures were nothing like this grand reality. If I had been consulted at the creation of the world, I should have placed Paradise here, in this very region."

"Ah, you haven't been here long yet," remonstrated Olaf, although he was secretly rejoiced at her enthusiasm. "But if you had to stay here in the winter, when the wind drives huge drifts of black cloud in between the mountains, and this calm glittering fjord is one vast mass of dark foamy smoke, and the leafless trees bend and moan under the scourge of the tempest, then I am afraid you would change your opinion."

"But then one appreciates a warm and cosy parlor the more; and if I could only have the monthly magazines and all the reading matter I wanted, I don't think it would be so terrible."

"Who is romantic now?" exclaimed he laughingly. "Don't you remember how you ridiculed me in Strasbourg for this same sort of talk?"

"Oh yes; that was in Strasbourg, you know," retorted she. "But now we are in Norway, and that makes quite a difference."

Where the highway bordered on the beach, there grew a couple of drooping birches, between which there was a rough bench. It was rather large for one, and would seat two without much difficulty. Ruth and Olaf, found the spot peculiarly inviting. It was high tide; the mirror of the water moved in smooth, pensive undulations which caught a tinge of crimson from the sunset, became transparent as they neared the shore, and broke in a soft ripple upon the sand. Large white sea-birds sailed calmly under the sky, then plunged headlong into the fjord, whence high spurts of spray rose and again fell hissing over the shining surface. Olaf had never felt prouder of his native land than in this moment;

and the fact that Ruth deemed it worthy of her admiration heightened a hundredfold his own enjoyment. The enchantment of her presence filled the air, and made it sweeter and richer to breathe. The dreamy apathy which had possessed him before her arrival had vanished, and the bright atmosphere which ever surrounded her, like a bracing breath of the sea, had awakened his senses to a keener delight in existence.

"Miss Ruth," he said at last, "I think I know you better now than I ever did before. These few hours have taught me—well, I hardly know what."

He was half prepared to have her ridicule the sentiment or even resent it; but to his surprise, she smiled in a pleased way, and answered, "*I* might with greater truth say the same of *you*. What appeared anomalous to me before, and often startled me, is now perfectly intelligible. Having learned to comprehend the country in which you have spent your early years, knowing the length of your stay in America, and then considering your natural disposition—supposing these three things to be known quantities, I think I could have calculated your character with the exactness of an algebraic problem—that is, if I had any head for mathematics," she added with a merry laugh. "But unfortunately I have not."

"Well, it is your good luck or my good luck—whatever you please—that you are not gifted in that direction," was his reply. "I should dislike to be such an inevitable result of certain iron forces in the making of which I had myself no hand. Moreover, I am persuaded that you cannot calculate human beings in that fashion."

"Yes, with men you can, but with women it is quite another matter. They are the results of a thousand incalculable combinations, which are too subtle for the mathematician to deal with. Therefore the attempt on the part of a man to account for the doings or the character of a woman always ends in dire failure."

"But do you mean to imply that women mutually understand each other?"

"At times. Yes."

"*Ergo:* women are greater mathematicians than men, and there our logic stops."

"How provokingly stubborn you are," cried

Ruth, and sprang up from her seat. "Now I think it is time that we commenced to talk about something else."

He was not in a mood to contradict her. She might have persisted that the grass was blue and the beach green, and he would joyfully have consented. The sea kept up its vague murmur in their ears; the song-thrush, the nightingale of Norway, warbled drowsily in the crowns of the birch-trees, and the arctic summer night shed its soft splendor around them. They walked slowly along the strand, now stopping to pick up a curious shell, now watching the flight of the large white-winged sea-birds.

"How do people know when to go to bed here?" said Ruth, lifting her eyes to the great sun-gilded peaks in the distance. "It must be past nine o'clock now, and it is almost as light as at noon. And still it is a different kind of light—as if the sun was a little bit weary, and was good-humoredly coaxed into staying up a little for our benefit. Somehow or other, I cannot get out of the notion that all this has been gotten up on my account, and that, as soon as I have become domesticated, nature will again assume its usual working-day appearance. I know it is unpardonably conceited in me to think so; but after all it is a pleasant conceit. So, why should I dismiss it?

"I can see no earthly reason why you should," answered Olaf. "Only wait a few days, and I will arrange a sunset among the glaciers for you, and, if possible, an avalanche which will sweep away a few peasants' houses, and some other theatrical effects of the same sort. I dare say you will enjoy it hugely, and you will probably never have such another experience in all your life."

At the garden gate they met Brynhild, who was just starting out in search of them.

"Grandmother was afraid you might be catching cold," she said, "and she wished me to bring you this shawl."

"Thank you," said Ruth; "there is no danger of my catching cold in this temperature. But if I can oblige anybody by putting on a shawl, I will do it."

Olaf and his sister exchanged a rapid glance;

both understood the old lady's tactics; but Ruth seemed to have no suspicion.

"But you didn't tell me how people know when to go to bed here," began Ruth. "If the sun keeps on at this rate, I shall be dreadfully mixed up about day and night."

"We go altogether by instinct. We go to bed when we are tired, and get up when we feel like it. And by a fortunate coincidence, we all get tired about the same time, and when Brynhild says that breakfast is on the table, we all have a simultaneous impulse to rise."

"What a delightful way of living. I have no doubt I shall soon get accustomed to it."

They walked up through the garden, and joined the group on the balcony. As the clock struck ten in the hall, the Judge rose, bade the company good night, and retired. The ladies soon followed his example. Olaf felt no desire for sleep; the great fact that Ruth had arrived so filled his mind that it left no room for any other thought. He lit a cigar and flung himself down in his grandfather's easy-chair. It was still light; but just the faintest suggestion of twilight (that clear, transparent twilight of the North) lingered in the air, and the sky was grave with nocturnal blue. It had been such a great day that the young man could not consent to go to rest before having somehow made clear to himself its meaning and summed up its possible results. That he loved Ruth—that was at least certain; he no longer feared to confess it to himself or even to her; and all the imagined difficulties of uncongeniality of disposition and interests, etc., which had so distressed him a month ago, had vanished in mist. And as he weighed the chances of Ruth's loving him, the thing did not at least seem such an utter absurdity as at the time when first he considered the question. In the light of this new possibility, Olaf Varberg hopefully viewed the life that lay before him. With a joyful tumult of heart, he saw the time when, sitting in his cosy study, he should find himself in the situation so charmingly described by Pliny in one of his letters. How lightly would not the winged thoughts flow under the spell of her presence; how good-naturedly would he not suffer those little interruptions when, leaning confidingly over the back of his chair, she would glance down on the page on which he was writing; and what wild throbs of happiness would not throng his bosom when he read her affectionate sympathy in her eyes, and that fine pride which only a wife can take in her husband's real or imagined greatness. All this he saw and felt, and the imaginary scene made him as happy as if he had merely to reach out his hand to make it real. Never had his duties to himself and to her appeared more sacred to him than in this moment; never had the talent, which he knew to be his, appeared such a great and glorious thing; never had his purpose in life been so strong and so clearly defined. In this little reverie he was disturbed by a pair of soft arms which were gently laid about his neck, and a warm cheek, which was lightly pressed against his. Olaf was too bewildered to think; he turned his head quickly, and a shade of disappointment flitted over his features. It was Brynhild.

"Ah, is it you?" he said, perhaps a little coldly.

Brynhild did not answer, but only wound her arms more tightly about his neck, as if she were afraid that somebody might come and tear him away from her. Presently he felt his cheek growing wet, and he discovered that she was weeping.

"But, my dear girl, what is the matter with you?" asked Olaf gently, drawing her down into his lap.

"Oh, how lovely, how beautiful she is." sobbed Brynhild, and hid her face on his bosom.

"Who is lovely? who is beautiful? I am sure I don't understand you."

"Ah, your American lady. You never told us that she looked like that."

"And you cry because she is lovelier and more beautiful than you imagined her?"

"Oh, Olaf, you don't know," cried the girl, with a fresh burst of grief. "We thought—Thora and I thought—that—that you would always remain at home."

She started up as if frightened at her own words, and almost ran into the house. Olaf hardly knew why, but her words sent a pang to his heart. His first impulse was to call after her and demand an explanation; but somehow he imagined what she might have to tell him, and on a second thought he concluded that there are times when certainty is even worse than doubt. So he arose and walked up to his rooms; but his happy reverie was spoiled.

Ruth woke up with the sensation of having slept for a fortnight when the maid called her the next morning. And when the shining coffee-pot was placed upon a little table before her bed, and the fragrant brown liquid poured into the china cups, she opened her eyes widely, and asked why they had allowed her to sleep until after dinner. She had a vague impression that the German custom of drinking coffee immediately on rising from the dinner-table prevailed in Norway too (as indeed it does); but the Norse fashion of drinking coffee while in bed she was as yet unacquainted with. But, as she had already declared, she was bound to respect the national customs; and to convince herself of her own sincerity, she began with making a martyr of herself by drinking more than she really wanted.

This old house, with its spacious halls, its quaint tapestry, and its air of good cheer and large-handed hospitality, had strangely wrought upon the young girl's fancy. And then this stately old gentleman, with his stiff gait and his old-fashioned *chivalresqueness* of manner, possessed a certain romantic fascination in her eyes; in her present mood she was half disposed to regret that Olaf's sojourn in her own land had made him so hopelessly American and so utterly disloyal to the traditions of his family. She liked the old Judge immensely, and was naturally anxious that he should like her. It was therefore no mere comedy on her part, when, on appearing for breakfast this morning, she professed a vivid interest in the family pictures and allowed their owner to conduct her through the gallery and entertain her with the history and incidents connected with each separate portrait. If she had artfully plotted the conquest of the old man, she could never have chosen a more ingenious method. And when Olaf, who had enjoyed a little nap after the coffee, entered the drawing-room, he observed the pleased expression in his grandfather's countenance, and secretly triumphed in Ruth's success. He was unjust to her, however, when in his heart he suspected her of design.

This vast, unrippled calm of the Northern sky, the serenely idyllic mood of the late summer, with its faint undulations of tone, by their very novelty imparted to Ruth's mind an ever-fresh sense of adventure. The days went by, but all limits of time and space were, as it were, blurred, and the question whether it was Sunday or Monday concerned her no more than did the household expenses of the Emperor of China. All she knew was that she thought this a most delightful way of living; and as long as her aunt showed no signs of impatience, she saw no reason why she should trouble herself about the morrow. The mornings were usually spent on the fjord, rowing or fishing; the afternoons were devoted to rambles through the neighboring birch grove; and in the evening the Judge and Ruth invariably had a "musical fight" about Chopin, Liszt, and Beethoven, which usually ended with a practical test of the merits of these composers. Ruth did play Chopin superbly. Those inarticulate sighs which at times seem to be struggling through the gloom-fraught chords of his nocturnes she rendered with a deep and powerful pathos, as if she had herself experienced all this dim yearning and sorrow and despair. The old man would on such occasions sit down at her side, at first intent upon finding fault, then gradually forgetting his hostile intentions, until his eyes kindled with sympathetic animation; and at last he would rise abruptly, and begin to pace up and down the floor. Ruth saw and enjoyed her triumph, but she was too prudent to take advantage of it; and the Judge, who was just a little bit stubborn, sat down once more and opened fire on Liszt, whom he attacked the more fiercely because he had tacitly admitted his defeat on Chopin. Then Ruth played one of the "Rhapsodies Hongroises," and there was another armistice. Nevertheless the Judge was by no means positive whether he approved or disapproved of this young American girl; he was sure that he admired her, but it was always under a protest. In his opinion women had no right to be so clever, so bright, and so self-possessed; in the good old times when he was young, girls never spoke unless they were addressed, and then they invariably blushed and answered, in trembling monosyllables; and a young man, when in the company of ladies, naturally assumed a slightly patronizing tone, and was in return agreeably impressed with the idea of his own importance. The Judge could not but smile when he imagined the way Ruth would meet a man who should approach her in this manner. Then, it was not to be denied, Ruth was an American, and America and revolution were to his mind identical terms. America had been his evil demon; it had sowed the seed of discord in his family, had deprived him of his only son, and now God only knew what was to happen. The Judge felt that it was his duty to dislike this young lady, and he did his best; but when he sat at her side, and saw the fine intelligence of her dark eyes, and listened to those bright little remarks of hers, which came and went like a flash of the Aurora Borealis, then he could only rebel in silence and own that resistance was vain. But Ruth was happily unconscious of all this: she came, saw, and conquered.

CHAPTER XIV.

The Glacier Expedition.

"THERE was once a princess, who was the most beautiful princess in all the world," exclaimed Olaf, as he saw Ruth emerging from her room with a fine, fresh color on her cheeks, and attired in the jaunty costume which with her aunt's aid she had improvised for the glacier excursion.

"And there was once a prince, who was the sauciest creature that ever lived," retorted Ruth, pushed him aside, and ran down stairs.

It was about six o'clock in the morning. A company of young people, including the youthful *élite* of all the neighborhood, had gathered down on the pier, and a couple of sturdy oarsmen, with yellow knee-breeches and red-peaked caps, were engaged in clearing the boats. Tea-kettles, lunch-baskets, and various articles of wearing apparel were stowed away under the row-benches, and the young lieutenants, who liked to display their authority before the ladies, shouted their orders in stentorian accents. Then all of a sudden there was a hush; the ladies put their heads together and spoke in whispers, and the gentlemen pulled at their waistcoats and drew themselves up into martial attitudes. Ruth was seen descending the garden terrace. They had all heard about this wonderful American beauty, but only few of them had seen her; rumor had been busy with her name even before her arrival, and had magnified every circumstance connected with her into the most fabulous dimensions. That she had come to marry the grandson of the Judge seemed to be a settled thing; and it was told for certain that she owned a bank of her own, and was rich enough to buy out the whole parish. The parish shoemaker, who was the authorized bearer of news, had reported her to be "fairer and richer than the Queen of England," taking it for granted that the Queen of England was beyond dispute, by virtue of her position, the most beautiful woman in the world. He had also thrown out some dark hint about "their doing things differently in America," which by the parish gossips had been variously construed; but neither Ruth nor Olaf would have been particularly flattered if they had known of the doubt which existed in the minds of many as to whether it was he or she who had assumed the aggressive part in the marriage question. It was natural enough that so mysterious a creature, even if she had not been so loudly heralded, should have excited the curiosity and wonder of the half-rustic neighbors; now she stood among them, but the halo of her rare Southern beauty and the fabulous land from which she hailed still seemed to remove her far out of their sphere. She smiled and greeted them in her own frank, friendly way, while they thronged forward to be introduced. Then they all took their seats in the boats, and the oarsmen thrust out from the pier.

The morning fog was just rising from the water, and drifted in fleecy fragments up along the sides of the mountains. Stray bits of meadow and wheat field lay glittering brightly with myriad dewdrops, wherever the sun had made a rift in the white veil of the mist. The fjord shone with a soft summer freshness, as if it had just awakened from a long and healthful sleep. On all sides the huge uncertain forms of snow-hooded peaks mirrored themselves in the cool ethereal deep. Hundreds of sea birds were already on the wing; the shrill-voiced gull sailed majestically over the wakes of the boats, and hardly twenty feet away the fearless, white-breasted gannet plunged headlong into the tide and left a patch of eddying bubbles where it had vanished. As the sun rose higher a light shiver ran over the surface of the water, and its faint undulations played in changing tints of reflected blue and cool luminous green.

By some chance Thora Haraldson had come to occupy the seat next to Ruth in the stern of one of the boats. Olaf sat upon a cross bench opposite, dividing his attention between the landscape and the company. As his eyes fell upon the fair group before him, the picturesque contrast between the two struck his artistic fancy, and presently he found himself critically comparing them and trying to account for their points of difference. How frail and almost insignificant looked this slender blue-eyed alpine maiden by the side of that tall, brilliant, and magnificent beauty. And somehow she seemed to be conscious of her own insignificance, for she looked with large innocent eyes up into Ruth's face, and an expression of child-like wonder was visible in her features. "Ah," philosophized Olaf, "it is the problem of my life which stands embodied before me. The one is the peaceful, simple life of the North, with its small aims and cares, its domestic virtues, and its calm, idyllic beauty. Love to her means duty, a gentle submissiveness, and the attachment bred by habit and mutual esteem. But in the other's bosom lives a world of slumbering tumult, a host of glorious possibilities, which though still shrunken in the bud, will one day, when touched by the wakening warmth of love, develop all the emotional wealth and grandeur of perfect womanhood. She is the flower of a larger and intenser civilization, and all the burning pulses of life which animate this great century, unknown to herself, throb in her being. And it is my own future which I love in her. I too shall become a larger and a more perfect man for what I give and what I receive in the mystery of such a love. The past lies behind me, and Ruth and love before me."

Olaf might have causd a sensation by proposing then and there, if Ruth had not unsciouly interrupted his reverie.

"Mr. Olaf," said she (for she too had got into the habit of calling him by that name because it sounded so delightfully barbarous), "these mountains don't always look so tall and magnificent, do they?"

"Oh, not by any means," retorted Olaf, who was in that moment capable of saying anything. "Don't you see they are standing on tiptoe looking over the edge of those clouds in order to catch a glimpse of you? It is not often that they have the chance of seeing such a sight."

"Now, don't be absurd, pray," answered she, and smiled, rather in spite of herself. "I really meant it quite seriously. I think you said something the other day about optical delusions caused by the singular transparency of the air at certain seasons of the year, or something of that sort."

"Yes," said Olaf, with a malicious twinkle in his eye; "I did say something of that sort. I said that when beautiful young ladies came here to visit them, the mountains suddenly remember their youthful dreams, and they have just enough of the dandy about them to make them anxious to produce a good impression. Therefore they wrap a picturesque cloak of sun-gilded mist about their shoulders, cock their glittering helmets of ice a little so as to look reckless, straighten their aged backs, and shake off the avalanches which slumbering centuries have heaped up there. And then—you would hardly believe it—strange tumultuous emotions awake in their stony breasts, and warm the huge masses of ice which have gathered in their beards; and the ice melts; boisterous cataracts rush down over their bosoms; their sombre armors of pine forest swell as if they were going to burst, and hoarse, rumbling noises issue forth from their glacial throats. Then they are only trying if they haven't lost their voices. That is how the mountains behave when they are in love. And you know, Miss Ruth, all this is not so absurd as it may sound to you; for when you have made conquests of grandfather, and Brynhild, and myself, and all the rest of us, why then should the mountains be exceptions?"

"Why, Mr. Olaf," cried Ruth laughingly,

"you are certainly fibbing. All this was not at all what you told me. But you do talk so magnificently. Pray go on. You may say whatever you please."

"But the trouble is I haven't got anything more to say."

"Well, then, you may keep quiet. But by the way, does your friend Miss Thora speak English?"

"I don't suppose she knows herself; probably she never tried."

"I do understand a little," said Thora timidly. "But I cannot speak."

"Then Mr. Olaf will act as our interpreter. Won't you, Mr. Olaf?"

"Oh, certainly."

And the conversation commenced. They talked of Norway and of America, of the wonders of fjords and glaciers, and of their own little private doings; but where the thoughts have to pass through the medium of an interpreter a conversation can never become confidential.

It was still early morning when the rowers, as if by mutual agreement, pulled up the dripping oars and poised them under their knees; the clear drops of water sparkled like sun-smitten emeralds, and fell with a sharp metallic click upon the shining surface. This was the usual resting-place, and Olaf, in deference to ancient custom, let a large jug of beer pass the round among his crew. There was a slight current perceptible, and the boats were allowed to drift; and as Ruth looked up she uttered a cry of surprise, and gazed in frightened wonder upon the vast panorama of desolation which spread out before her. A minute ago they had seen nothing but the huge promontory which loomed up straight before them, and which made them feel as if the boats in which they were sitting were mere nutshells. Now, as if the mountain wall had been raised like a back curtain in a theatre, the view suddenly deepened; the sunshine itself became suffused as it were with a bluish ice-tint, and as far as the eye could reach, the granite Titans of the primeval world raised their hoary heads in calm defiance of heaven. The keen arrows of the sun smote upon their shields of snow, and rebounded in brilliant reflections from their icy helmets, and the sombre shadows of the fjord below were startled with rapid flushes of crimson, gold, and violet.

"We are not going in there, are we?" said Ruth anxiously. "It looks to me as if the whole thing was coming down. I really doubt if it is safe to enter."

"My official duties compel me to travel here every week," remarked one of the lieutenants, who could speak a little English. "But it never occurred to me to be frightened."

"Ah," said Ruth, with a smile.

"Why should I be frightened?" continued the martial youth, anxious to follow up his triumph.

"No, I can't really see why you should," replied she. "I am sure *I* shouldn't."

The gentleman's countenance fell, and he hastened to volunteer his service at the oars. The boats had now entered a narrow branch of the fjord, one of the most wildly picturesque regions which Norway or any other country has to show. It looked like a mere narrow cleft between two gigantic chains of mountains which rose with a grand sweep, almost perpendicularly from the water. The bare steep sides were thickly furrowed with the tracks of avalanches, and at times, where the slope descended less abruptly, wildernesses of débris and water-carved bowlder rose like the stern mausoleums of dead glaciers. Ruth was right—it did seem as if the mountains might at any moment take it into their heads to close this rift, which evidently some earthquake or similar revolution had burst open while the earth was still young and enthusiastic. The company spoke in whispers, as if they were afraid of waking some slumbering Trold, whose very breath might be fraught with destruction. The old Norse legends of St. Olaf and the giants seem very credible things in a scene like this.

Toward noon the boats were put in at a little pier, where a boisterous torrent mingled its passionate voice with the noonday silence of the fjord. A low growth of stunted birch and alder trees edged its banks, and large flocks of goats were scattered through the bottom of the broad ravine.

To the westward shone the vast expanse of eternal snow; a mighty arm of this illimitable arctic field shot down through this very cleft, the upper end of which it filled like a huge wedge of silver.

"Now, here is a chance for your optical illusions," said Olaf, as he stood with Ruth on the strand. "How long do you suppose it would take you to walk up to the edge of that glacier?"

"I should imagine about ten minutes," answered she unsuspectingly.

"If you walk that distance in less than three-quarters of an hour, I will pledge myself to climb the peak over there in the same time."

Ruth laughed, and appealed to the lieutenant, who, with outrageous disregard for her feelings, decided that she might regard herself as lucky if she reached the spot at all, and that an hour was the minimum of time required. The gentlemen were then called upon to assist in unloading the boats, and Ruth, who was beginning to feel the cold breath of the glacier, allowed Olaf to wrap a shawl about her, and sat down with Thora on the bank of the stream. There was a brief debate whether they should serve the dinner here or up under the ice field, and as the sun shone brightly up there, while the bottom of the cleft was filled with shadow, the latter plan finally prevailed. Olaf now began to feel his responsibility as host and, at his sister's suggestion, during the upward march devoted himself equally to all the ladies. They were all very nice, some even pretty, but although many of them had known him in his boyhood, they seemed reluctant to recognize in this tall, bearded gentleman the gay and light-hearted youth who wrote verses and was the lion of the parish balls five years ago. Then his dress was of a foreign cut, and there was still a perceptible accent in his speech. To be sure, he was perfectly frank and friendly with them, but for all that, his foreign sojourn had raised up an insurmountable wall between him and them, and if he had been attempting to talk to them across the Atlantic Ocean the distance could not have appeared greater. And Olaf, whose spiritual organism was as sensitive as that of a mimosa, was with every moment more impressed with his own strangeness, until at last he was inclined to look upon himself as a rhinoceros or some rare animal escaped from a menagerie.

The ascent of the steep ravine soon told on the strength of the ladies. Only Ruth kept bravely in the front with her lieutenant, and her merry laughter and her endurance stimulated the ambition of the rest. The rugged path lay along the edge of the glacier torrent, which roared and foamed a hundred feet below, and occasionally sent up a fierce gust of cold, shivering spray. Rude piles of erratic bowlder, interspersed with solitary bushes of birch and juniper, covered the sides of the ravine, and away toward the west lay a huge mass of billowy ice, like a cataract of molten silver suddenly congealed or by some magic agency arrested in its course. It was an hour past noon when the merry company halted under the brink of the glacier. Olaf hastened to Ruth's side. He was curious to see how this sight would impress her.

"What a fierce, wicked, terrible thing this is," said she gravely, gazing on the wall of earth and stone which the ice was pushing before it.

"Well, such things must be," remarked Olaf philosophically.

"Now, don't you laugh at me," continued Ruth in the same serious tone; "but do you really think that these grand monstrosities were in the original plan of creation? Or do you believe that they are accidental things which have somehow been developed afterward? I really can't see the use of them."

"I am afraid I am not enough of a naturalist to tell what their special use may be in the cosmic economy," replied he. "But from an æsthetic point of view it is easy to account for their existence. You know, beauty is its own excuse for being, as Emerson says, and you will certainly not deny that this glacier is beautiful."

"No; to be sure, it is beautiful," said the girl. "But it is a beauty which makes me tremble. There is something hard, and fierce, and cruel in it. It is the same sort of beauty that there is in a thunderstorm, and I am afraid I am not heroic enough to enjoy it."

Indeed there *is* a suggestion of terror and of stern demoniac will in these frozen masses of wintry strength, and even the glory of a hundred sunsets could not lend one tinge of serener beauty to their cold, fierce sentiment of divine grandeur and wrath. It is the God of the Old Testament who dwells in the glaciers, and whose voice makes itself heard in the midnight terror of their avalanches.

The arctic sun, which even on a midsummer noonday is far from the zenith of the sky, was slowly journeying to the westward, and soon stood almost behind the glacier. At a few miles' distance, where its upper ridges touched the sky, an army of sparkling steeples traced itself airily upon the near horizon, while further toward the north, where the plateau sloped downward, and the outline of the ice seemed less jagged, the boundless snow fields sent forth a vast blinding glare which pained the eye beyond endurance. But it was a joy to watch the manifold play of the light upon the colossal ridges, as they loomed skyward, and again abruptly descended in labyrinthine lines toward the wall of *moraine* which bounded the lower plateau. Through their thin, gracefully sculptured edges, as keen as that of a billow in the act of breaking, shone a glittering maze of delicate, star-shaped frost-flowers, and gradually, as the ice-blocks became thicker and more opaque, their color shaded through all the paler tints of blue into the deepest sapphire gloom. And looking upward over the crests of this whole *mer de glace*, a strange shimmering sheen, like the ghosts of a thousand disembodied colors, seemed to be floating in the air, struggling to rise, but by some hidden power to be fettered to the icy billows.

The more prosaic part of the company had, in the meanwhile, been engaged in spreading the dinner, upon some large blocks of stone about fifty feet distant from the ice-wall. The charge of the Judge's portable wine cellar Olaf willingly surrendered to one of the officers. A rude fireplace was built, the unopened lunch baskets ransacked, and the guests seated in picturesque little groups upon a grassplot near the banks of the river. The sun was blazing bright and warm, and what little wind there was blew toward the glacier; so the spirits of the young people gradually thawed; the shy little maidens laughed and chattered, and the martial gentlemen joked amiably, and recounted their hunting and camp adventures. When the dinner was at an end, Olaf startled the company by announcing his intention of ascending the glacier. He first asked the gentlemen if any of them was disposed to accept his guidance, as he knew the topography of the place from his boyhood; and when they refused, he appealed to the ladies. The fair-haired damsels stared as if he had requested them to take a balloon voyage with him; but still greater was their wonder when Ruth rose and said that she would be glad to put herself under his charge.

"But I warn you beforehand that it is no joking matter," said Olaf, who was perhaps himself somewhat startled; "there are continually loose blocks breaking away, and you know the guide-books say that the ascent from this side is dangerous."

"Oh, I have thick boots on," answered she, with a critical glance at her feet, "and as for the rest, it can be no more dangerous to me than to you."

"You are the bravest girl that ever lived," whispered he in her ear. "I am charmed to have your company."

"Hypocrite!" laughed she. "Your face tells a different story. But for all that, I am bound to keep you to your word."

The young Norseman, used from his earliest boyhood to mountain climbing, felt his heart leap within him at the glorious prospect of a stroll over the eternal snow fields, with this fair maiden of Southland birth. For to the arctic fancy of a Norwegian, the name of America is fragrant with the perfume of tropic vegetation and southern romance; and although Olaf had spent four winters in New England, he made no effort to rid himself for the time being from his early hallucinations. He relieved Ruth of her shawls, gave her his hand, and struck in upon the path along the northern side of the ice-field.

"And when can we expect you back?" cried Brynhild after them.

"We are not going to mount to the top," shouted he; "and if we are not back in an hour and a half, you will never see us again, at least not in the condition in which we departed."

Brynhild looked frightened; but she knew that her brother had always had his own way, and that it would be of no use to interfere. Ruth was not altogether unpractised in climbing; she had had a brief experience a month ago in the Saxon Switzerland, and she now frequently astonished her guide by the accuracy with which she measured a distance wherever there was occasion for a leap. The path crept with irregular steeps and windings along the edge of the glacier, now and then losing itself in devious "goat tracks" whenever a pile of scattered rocks necessitated a departure from the ice-line. But Olaf never hesitated in his course, and Ruth had perfect confidence in his guidance. It was a wonder to him that this girl, who had complained of weariness when they ascended the Strasbourg Cathedral could step so briskly through this stony wilderness, never losing her foothold, and without a murmur of complaint. He put it down mentally as another enigma of the feminine character. But this keen, bracing mountain air has a wonderfully stimulating effect. He already felt the magic of its breath in the vigorous rush of his own blood, and in Ruth's cheeks it had kindled a glow of deeper color. There was fire in her eye, and her voice had a rich and joyous ring, born, as he fancied, of the splendor and the excitement of the hour. After more than half an hour's climb they reached a sheltered nook where a slender, sparsely-leafed birch, frail as a frost-flower, stood trembling over the glacial abyss. From hence they made a cautious excursion out on the ice, and again returned to take a few moments' rest. Here in the lee of a projecting rock and exposed to the southern sun, some faintly-tinted alpine flowers had been coaxed into life, and Olaf plucked them, gave them to Ruth, and indulged in a little reverie about their brief and joyless existence. Ruth was in a sympathetic mood. She met his thought half way and instinctively caught it before it was uttered. The vast loneliness and the dread desolation which surrounded them seemed to bring them nearer together. There was to him at that moment no woman in all the world except Ruth; he and she had been chosen to inhabit and to rule the virgin earth. Far down in the unseen deep rushed and booned the subterranean glacier torrents, like the voces of eternity. And in his own heart pulsed a kindred life, and a voice as mighty and eternal sang in his own breast the ever fresh mystery of creation.

"Mr. Olaf," said she, bending compassionately over the flowers, "do you think these poor shivering little things are really alive. They seem to me the mere frozen breath of the glacier. Excuse me; I grow poetical without knowing it."

"You need make no excuses," answered he, and seated himself at her side under the birch tree. "To be sure, I should call it a mere semblance of life. And so are the lives of thousands of men and women who eke out their existence here in the constant struggle for daily bread. What do they know of what life has to offer?"

"But they seem healthy and robust enough?"

"Yes; but they count their years by winters."

"How strange. And did you too, when you lived here, say that you were so and so many winters old?"

"Yes, I did. But from the time I saw you, Ruth, mine has been a summer life, and henceforth I shall number my age by its summers. It all depends upon you, Ruth," he added in a passionate whisper. "I love you."

A terrible crash was heard. A fierce, splitting noise shot through the glacier, and a huge block of ice broke loose and tumbled down into the abyss, startling the silent air with a harsh, continuous peal, as of receding thunder. Ruth gave a frightened cry, and in the bewilderment of terror flung her arms around Olaf's neck and clung fast to him. He sat calm, and did not stir from the spot; in the excitement of that moment nothing could have moved or surprised him. The dread thunder of the glacier seemed but the fitting accompaniment to his declaration. He quietly stooped down over the girl, gazed into her frightened face, and kissed her. Then it suddenly occurred to him that it might merely have been her fright which had involuntarily brought her into his embrace, and that possibly he had been ungenerous in taking advantage of her agitation. This suspicion drove the blood to his face; he swiftly released her from his arms, and stammered something about mistakes and excuses. The girl, who was now perfectly composed, opened her eyes wide in astonishment; then the ludicrous side of the situation suddenly struck her.

"Why, Olaf," she cried, "don't be *too* conscientious, pray. If it is a mistake, it is at all events rather late to retreat now. We shall have to stand by it like heroes."

"Ruth," exclaimed he, with a happy laugh, "you are incorrigible. To joke in a place and in a moment like this!"

The mention of the place started a fresh fear in her mind.

"You don't suppose they can see us from down there?" exclaimed she, and sprang up from her seat.

"What if they do?" answered he composedly.

"Not for all the world," said she fiercely. "I would rather die than have them see us."

"Well, calm yourself then. If they had the eyes of Argus, they could not see through that rock."

The stillness of the wilderness grew with every moment intenser; the cold white face of the glacier settled into something like a frown, and the icy sheen upon its brow rose with a sterner glare against the azure sky. To be sure, summer had invaded its domain; what was more natural than that it should resent it? It was probably a novel experience for the glacier to have this glowing bit of summer, with its thousand warm suggestions (one of which would be enough to thaw an iceberg), nestled here on its very bosom. Something like this Olaf would undoubtedly have thought, as he stood silently regarding the glacier before beginning the descent, if he had not just then been too happy to have any thought at all. A vast, shapeless bliss filled his being. It seemed such an inconceivable privilege to be able to call Ruth by her first name, leaving out the "Miss;" and during the delightful rambling talk which they carried on, as long as the wilderness alone could hear them, he frequently had to restrain himself for fear of betraying how boyish he was in his glee. He had always somehow had the idea that the whole masculine sex were pining for Ruth, and he could not but confess to himself that a sense of triumph over his unsuccessful brethren added to the keenness of his joy. A loud chorus of voices welcomed them as they reached the bottom of the ravine, and as it was already late in the afternoon, they rested but a few minutes and then continued their march to the fjord. Brynhild whispered something to her brother about monopolizing the American lady, and he, in return, stared blankly at her, as if he could not quite see what she meant, and then burst out into an uncontrollable fit of laughter. He had in one way or another to give vent to his superabundant spirits, and this presented the first occasion.

"And, after all, we did have the pleasure of seeing you again in the same condition in which you departed," said one of the lieutenants to Olaf, as the boats were thrust out from the beach.

"No; I beg your pardon," answered he thoughtlessly; "my condition has been considerably changed by that glacier climb."

"Ah," said the lieutenant, and raised his eyebrows significantly.

A quick blush sprang to Ruth's face, and she sent Olaf an imploring glance.

"Yes," continued he, in the same careless voice; "it has been an experience which probably" (with a mischievous glance at Ruth) "I shall never have the chance of repeating. It has increased my store of knowledge, and given me a glimpse of a side of the divine economy with which I never expected to become acquainted."

"And with us, you know, we have no glaciers at all," interposed Ruth energetically.

"Oh, yes, I understand," remarked the martial gentleman, with a disappointed look; "it must have been a very interesting experience—although a very cold one, I should judge," he added, shivering.

Olaf was about to answer, but Ruth promptly stopped him.

"You turned that very neatly," whispered she, and smiled approvingly, as an hour later they sat side by side in the stern of the boat.

The sun sank below the horizon, the daylight faded, and the golden crescent of the moon rose from behind a snow-clad peak. It shed its pale glimmer upon the water, which shone with changing tints, playing between steel blue and the usual lucid green. The evening was calm; hardly a ripple moved the mirror of the fjord, save those evanescent undulations which spread from the bows of the boats. The young officers, who had good voices, sang the famous Swedish duets "Gluntarne," and the clear-toned echoes of the mountains set the solemn, remote wildernesses a-trembling with joyous melody. It was within an hour of midnight when they landed at the Judge's pier. The hospitable mansion was prepared for their reception. Only a few of the ladies followed Thora to be the guests of the Colonel.

"What are you doing there, Ruth?" asked Olaf, as after some search he found his heroine standing behind the curtain in one of the recesses of the windows.

"Oh, it is—it is only those glacier flowers," answered she (and it was the first time in his life that he had seen her confused); "those flowers which reckoned their age by winters. Oh, Olaf," she exclaimed, suddenly interrupting herself, "tell me truly and honestly, don't you think me dreadfully heartless?"

"Heartless!" ejaculated he, as if such a thing had never entered his head; "how can you imagine anything so absurd?"

"Well, it *isn't* absurd," persisted the girl vehemently. "I came to think of it to-day. I hardly believe that I have said one friendly word to you since we became acquainted. But for all that you may be sure of one thing," she added in a hushed, earnest tone, "and that is that I love you."

The moon sailed swiftly through the nocturnal sky, the rising tide beat faintly against the strand—but Ruth and Olaf still lingered in the curtained recess at the window.

CHAPTER XV.

Conclusion.

FOR two days Ruth and Olaf were successful in preserving the secrecy of their engagement, but at the end of that time they both tacitly, if not openly, admitted that for a self-imposed duty it was a very arduous one. Ruth had originally stipulated a week, and had even had serious thoughts of a fortnight. And when her lover was unable to see the expediency of all her feminine diplomacy, and even ventured to grumble, she would disarm him with a smile, and then add in her own bewitching way, "Well, you know, it is an admirable thing for discipline."

But to-day Ruth had herself twice fallen out of her rôle; first at the breakfast table she had called him by his first name, and an hour ago, as he stood talking with his grandfather out on the balcony, she had come up from behind, put her arm through his, and gazed into his face with a sort of absent-minded tenderness, which would have been sufficiently convincing to the old gentleman, if he had not been too much interested in the discussion to notice her. Brynhild's suspicions had been aroused long ago; and the soft joyous radiance of Ruth's eyes, the deep abstraction of her look when she thought herself unobserved, and even the occasional abruptness of her motions, all went to confirm her fears, and often made her waver in her allegiance to the fair-haired Thora, who was to have rebound the broken link and once more reconciled the exile to his family and his country.

But there was something about Ruth which somehow made it seem a privilege to be allowed to worship her; and Brynhild's loyal nature could not resist this influence; moreover, she loved her brother too well not to feel an intense interest in the woman who apparently held his fate in her hand. So these two soon became friends, and many a time Ruth's secret hovered upon her lips, and it was merely by virtue of an almost superhuman effort that she stayed her eager tongue. Brynhild, on the other hand, felt an equally irresistible desire to confide in Ruth the early marriage plot with Thora, but on a second thought she concluded that it would be ungenerous and cruel, and she forbore. Indeed, as the days went by, and she read in Ruth's dark eyes the tale which they would fain have hidden, and as she weighed the strong womanly fervor of a love like hers against the pale dreamy devotion of a nature like Thora's, she no longer wondered at her brother's choice.

The heavy red curtains had been drawn before the parlor windows; the evening was cloudy and a pleasant twilight filled the room. The Judge and his wife had just retired; Mrs. Elder had been suffering with a headache during the afternoon, and had not left her room since supper. Ruth was sitting at the piano, playing carelessly a bit of Schumann's Slumber-Song. Olaf had thrown himself into a corner of the sofa.

"Ruth," he said, "won't you please stop making that noise and come and sit down here? I have something important to tell you."

Ruth stopped in the middle of a measure,

wheeled round on the piano stool, and went to the sofa.

"Ruth," began he (for he still gloried in her name), "I have been very much worried to-day by the thought of what grandfather will say when he hears of this affair of ours. You know that both he and grandmother have set their hearts on keeping me at home. And I never mentioned that possibility to you, I think."

"I have thought of that possibility, nevertheless," said she seriously.

"And what have you thought, dear?"

"I have thought that I would consent to live even in Siberia, if you would only live there with me."

"Well, it was merely a supposititious case. You may be sure I want to live nowhere but in America."

And he went on to explain to her his position in his grandfather's house, reviewed the family history from the very beginning, and ended with declaring that he would go to the old Judge to-morrow, tell him of his engagement, and offer to renounce his inheritance. Ruth entered enthusiastically into this plan, and saw with secret pride the heroic figure Olaf would cut when stepping forward to propose this magnanimous sacrifice.

"But," she added, checking herself abruptly, "how much do you suppose your grandfather is worth?"

"Ruth, I am ashamed of you," cried he laughing. "Who would have believed that you were such a worldly creature. You approve of the principle abstractly, but when you come to its application in your own case or in mine, then you begin to have doubts—"

"You didn't answer my question, sir," interrupted she earnestly.

"Well, grandfather is probably worth about one hundred and twenty thousand dollars, of which one half would fall to me."

"But that is a great deal of money, Olaf; only think how many nice things we could buy for it."

Olaf instead of an answer flung his arms about her, and if the journal be correct, I am not sure but that their lips met by chance in the the twilight. Then a sharp click was heard in the next room, as if a key was being turned in the lock, which was followed by approaching footsteps. Ruth sprang up, as if she had been shot, rushed to the looking-glass, and began vigorously to smooth her hair, which had become somewhat disarranged. In an instant the door was opened, and the young girl in her bewilderment slipped behind the window curtain. Unhappily the Judge had an exceedingly sensitive ear, and the unfinished melody of the Slumber-Song had been haunting him for the last half-hour, and prevented him from falling asleep. Now he appeared, wrapped in his embroidered dressing-gown, sat quietly down at the piano, took up the air in the very measure where Ruth had been interrupted, and played it to the end. Olaf crouched down in the sofa, and in his heart he wished his grandfather a hundred miles away. But by an unlucky accident the old gentleman had confirmed himself in the habit of examining fire-places and window fastenings a couple of times before going to bed; and, as he rose from the piano, an evil destiny led him to the very window where Ruth had sought a hiding-place. The Judge drew the curtain gently aside.

"But, my dear," exclaimed he in a voice of

surprise, "are you playing hide-and-seek here, all alone?"

Ruth felt her heart beating in her throat; but she nerved herself for the moment, put on an air of reckless defiance, and stood bolt upright before the Judge. Olaf perceived that it was time for him to come to her rescue.

"Grandfather," he began bravely, taking Ruth by the hand, "Ruth and I—well, the fact is—that Ruth and I have found out that we love one another."

"Ruth and you have found out that you love one another, have you?" repeated the Judge slowly, as if he were weighing each word. "When did you find that out?"

"I discovered my love for Ruth a long time ago; the very first time I saw her."

"And I did too—a very long time ago," echoed Ruth eagerly.

"I can readily believe that," said the old man smiling, and seated himself on the piano stool. "He probably behaved in such a way that you must have been blind if you did not see it."

"You know I don't mean that," retorted the

girl, who felt her spirits rapidly reviving. "I am sure you understand very well what I do mean."

"Well, well," sighed the Judge; "young folks will make strange discoveries in this world."

Then there was a long pause, during which the Judge's breathing was painfully audible.

"Well," he said, raising his head abruptly, "what can I do about it? You haven't asked my advice, and I am sorry that I have disturbed you."

"We just want you to say that it is all right," answered Ruth promptly.

"You want me to say that it is all right. Aha! But now, if I should say that it isn't all right, what then?"

"Then we should be very sorry indeed."

"Yes, we should never be perfectly happy if we thought that we had grieved you," added Olaf.

"I would not make you unhappy for anything, children," said his grandfather, struggling hard to keep his voice firm. "However, I know that I can do but little here. You, my boy, have long been beyond my reach. And I know that it must be so, and accept what is inevitable. Since you wish my consent in this matter, I should be a wretch if I withheld it. I wish you all the happiness that life has to offer."

He rose quickly and went to the door. There he paused for a minute, and regarded with a sad eye the young couple, who still stood hand in hand before him in the twilight.

"Well, my dear," he said, taking a step toward Ruth, "if you are my daughter, I probably have the privilege of kissing you good night."

Ruth rushed toward him, and flung her arms about his neck. And he kissed her tenderly, as he would have kissed his own daughter; but a tear trembled in his eye—trembled for a moment, and fell on the girl's forehead.

What remains of Ruth's and Varberg's story may be briefly told, especially as the entries in the latter's journal after this date are few and irregular. They had a hard battle to fight the next day with Olaf's grandmother, but when she had convinced herself that resistance was vain, and moreover the Judge took sides against her, she gracefully succumbed, on the condition that she should herself have the privilege of making the wedding. Olaf remarks that since the engagement was made public, his grandfather has evinced a most extraordinary interest in America, and the grand republic furnishes inexhaustible themes for conversation at breakfast, dinner, and supper. It is also evident that the Judge takes no little pride in exhibiting his accomplished American daughter-in-law to the grandees of the parish. Old Mrs. Varberg, who regards her husband as an oracle, is also gradually relenting. Mrs. Elder has at last become convinced that the Norwegians are not identical with the Laplanders.

The last three entries I prefer to quote in the language of my original.

September 10.—To-day we received a cable telegram from Ruth's father. He intends to start with a Cunarder to-morrow, and promises to be here in time for the wedding.

September 12.—There is a rumor afloat, that Colonel Haraldson has promised his daughter to Lieutenant P——, who writes in grandfather's office.

September 15.—Yesterday grandmother made

a large party for Ruth and me. Half the parish was invited, and Ruth thinks it was a very magnificent affair. Grandfather gave the toast, which he ended with these words; "And now may God bless you, my children, be it in Norway or in America." I translated the speech in a whisper to Ruth, and she thought it wonderfully eloquent. It was very different from the way grandfather used to talk about America before she came, and she gloried the more in the change because she naturally assumed to herself the credit of having converted him.

THE END.

www.ingramcontent.com/pod-product-compliance
Lightning Source LLC
Chambersburg PA
CBHW032045230426
43672CB00009B/1473